Worl  e
by Hur r

Humphrey Spender was born in 1910. He trained as an architect, but turned to photography to make his living during the Depression. In the mid-thirties, he worked as the *Daily Mirror*'s 'Lensman'; and later he became one of the first photographers for *Picture Post*. In 1937-38, he took many hundreds of photographs for Mass-Observation.

Mass-Observation was set up in 1937, to collect first-hand information on all aspects of the lives of ordinary people in Britain. A major project was the study of Bolton – 'Worktown' – and as part of this, a number of well-known artists were invited to provide their own kinds of record of Bolton and its 'leisure extension', Blackpool. Today, Humphrey Spender's photographs are the most famous result.

Worktown People contains over a hundred photographs printed especially for this book, almost all of them by Humphrey Spender himself. The high standard of reproduction means that the quality of the originals has been caught to an unusual degree. The main part of the accompanying text consists of material taken from a series of interviews with Humphrey Spender about his life and work. It includes not only an account of what shaped his view of the world and of photography in the thirties, but also details of his working procedures.

To David and Quentin

Worktown People

Photographs from Northern England 1937-38

by Humphrey Spender

edited by Jeremy Mulford

FALLING WALL PRESS

Worktown People published by Falling Wall Press

First published February 1982

Photographs Copyright © 1982 Humphrey Spender in association with the Tom Harrisson Mass-Observation Archive
Introduction Copyright © 1982 Jeremy Mulford
Interview Copyright © 1982 Humphrey Spender and Jeremy Mulford
Notes Copyright © 1982 Harry Gordon, Humphrey Spender, the Tom Harrisson Mass-Observation Archive and Jeremy Mulford

Designed by Jill Coote, DP Press Ltd., Sevenoaks, Kent
Typeset by Type Practitioners Ltd., Sevenoaks, Kent
Printed by John S. Speight Ltd., Guiseley, Leeds, a division of Hawthornes of Nottingham Ltd.

Subsidised by the Arts Council of Great Britain

ISBN 0 905046 20 X

Falling Wall Press Ltd.
9 Lawford Street, Old Market, Bristol BS2 0DH, England

Acknowledgements

Suzie Fleming not only helped to edit the interview transcripts, but was the main source of advice for the book. As well as providing many of the Notes, Harry Gordon identified photographs about which we were doubtful and saved us from a number of errors. David Mellor and photographer Derek Smith organised in 1977 the original *Worktown* exhibition of Humphrey Spender's photographs, which began its life at the Gardner Centre, University of Sussex, and which was largely responsible for bringing these photographs to public notice after nearly forty years of obscurity. Unfortunately, illness prevented David Mellor from contributing to this book. Ernest Mulford took charge of most of the transcription of the interview tapes. Shirley Read and other members of the Half Moon Photography Workshop selected material from the Mass-Observation Archive for their travelling exhibition of *Worktown* photographs, and made this material freely available to us. Stella Robinson and Jill Coote of DP Press and Denis Hobson and Kenneth Jackson of Speight's coped with an exacting production schedule with great care and patience. Dorothy Sheridan, archivist at the Mass-Observation Archive, gave us much advice and other help. Jan Siegieda interrupted his preparation of the Arnolfini Gallery travelling exhibition of Humphrey Spender's photographs to do a number of prints for the book. Julian Trevelyan gave us permission to use the quotations from his book, *Indigo Days*. The Arts Council of Great Britain made a grant towards the production of the book; and Eastern Arts Association made a grant to Humphrey Spender towards the cost of making the prints. We are very grateful to all the above, and also to the following for help of various kinds: Richard Broad, John Dewhirst, Martin Forster, Martin Hobson, Judith Mathew, Ivy Mulford, Digby Norton, Wendy Ogden.

H.S. & J.M.

Contents

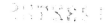

Mass-Observation is an independent, scientific, fact-finding body, run from 82, Ladbroke Road, London, W.11. (Part 6517.) It has a team of trained, whole-time objective investigators and a nation-wide panel of voluntary informants.

For five years it has documented the processes of social change, of political trend, of public and private opinion, in a series of books, bulletins, broadcasts and articles. It is concerned only:

1 with ascertaining the facts as accurately as possible;
2 with developing and improving the methods for ascertaining these facts;
3 with disseminating the ascertained facts as widely as possible.

Mass-Observation does not believe that social science can effectively operate only at the academic level. Its job is to study real life; and the people it studies are people who can be interested immediately in the results, which often directly concern their everyday lives.

Since it began with a handful of people and without any money Mass-Observation has become internationally known and recognized. Many political, social, commercial and official bodies have used it, in peace and war.

The Pub and the People (1943) page 2

Mass Observation was really the product of three minds, each seeking from it something different, each contributing to it a different technique. Besides Tom [Harrisson], its founders were Humphrey Jennings and Charles Madge. To Humphrey [Jennings], it was an extension of his Surrealist vision of Industrial England; the cotton workers of Bolton were the descendants of Stephenson and Watt, the dwellers in Blake's dark satanic mills reborn into a world of greyhound racing and Marks & Spencer. He had filmed them, and now he was to fix their irrational behaviour in another medium; it was his '1937ness' as André Masson had been his '1931ness'. His interest was intense but not long-lived.

To Charles Madge, who was now married to Kathleen Raine and lived in a beautiful eighteenth-century house at Blackheath, Mass Observation was a new kind of poetry. It was chiefly he who collated the 'reports' sent in each month by voluntary observers all over the country; who would choose out a description of five minutes in a country bus by a working girl, and hold it up for all the world to see, to savour the poetic overtones in those few casual words. Underneath, I believe, Charles was an empirical Marxist who wanted to understand the motives of individuals and to equate them with his own beliefs.

Tom however was the man of action, the anthropologist with the note-book. Not for Tom the eighteenth-century house on Blackheath, but rather the working-class house in Worktown, anonymous, and like those on either side of it. He complained to me at this time that he could not really sleep unless he could feel through the wall the people next door going to bed; could not work unless the radio was turned on full blast. Tom went out for his material to the pubs, to the dogs, to the dance halls. He sent a band of willing workers flying round making reports on anything, from the contents of a chemist's shop window to an account of a service in a spiritualist church. 'Bring back a list of hymns and any other dope you can get hold of, and try and pinch a copy of the sermon,' he would say as he sent us on our mission. For Tom had an almost hypnotic power over those who worked for him: he would ask the most impossible things of us and we would willingly do them.

Julian Trevelyan, *Indigo Days* (1957) pages 81-3

Introduction

Mass-Observation

The photographs in this book would not have been taken had it not been for the existence of Mass-Observation, which was founded in 1937. Humphrey Spender was invited to go to Bolton as part of the 'Worktown' project, set up to record everyday life in a Northern industrial town. On the opposite page are two accounts of Mass-Observation. The first is an 'official' version; the second, an affectionately reductive version, by an artist who was briefly caught up in the phenomenon. Both contain much that is true; and each substantially qualifies the other. But it would be wrong to suggest that the truth lies somewhere 'in between'. Julian Trevelyan's account itself suggests why this is so. For Mass-Observation's operation involved much haphazardness and many contradictions.

The two principal founders of Mass-Observation – Charles Madge, journalist and poet, and Tom Harrison, ornithologist and anthropologist – differed from each other in many respects, but they shared a preoccupation with how 'little we know of our next door neighbour and his habits; how little we know of ourselves. Of conditions of life and thought in another class or another district, our ignorance is complete. The anthropology of ourselves is still only a dream.'[1] Their preoccupation was with an absence of knowledge, coupled with the gross distortions of working-class life and opinion to be found everywhere in the press.

The extent of Mass-Observation's work is indicated by a passage in Tom Harrison's first report to the Vice-Chancellor of Sussex University, where all the material collected between 1937 and 1949* is now housed: 'The *quantity* is there for all to see, though at present an undigestible and largely unclassified bulk of massive raw paper. This bulk includes tens, no hundreds, of thousands of pages of nationwide and often pretty random observations and conversations, on many themes, several years'

intensive field work in Bolton ("Worktown"), monthly reports submitted over up to thirteen years by members of the panel of 1,500 men and women voluntary mass-observers, the day to day diaries kept by some 500 observers over these years – and much else'.[2]

The sort of data that Charles Madge's 'literary' approach produced is exemplified classically by the diary of Nella Last, the Barrow-in-Furness housewife who responded to Mass-Observation's invitation to 'ordinary people' to send them regular accounts of their lives and opinions by writing a voluminous, intimate diary for nearly thirty years.**

On the other hand, Tom Harrisson had been an anthropologist in Borneo and the New Hebrides, and in 1936 he decided that he wanted to be a field anthropologist in his own country. He chose to be this in Bolton ('Worktown', as he came to call it) because of what it 'shares in common with other principal working-class and industrial work-places throughout Britain';[3] and specifically because 'William Lever was born in Park Street, Worktown'.[4] Lever – who became Lord Leverhulme – provided a link between Tom Harrisson's two areas of interest: 'What was there of Western civilisation which impacted into the tremendously independent and self-contained culture of those cannibal people on their Melanesian mountain? Only one thing, significantly, in the mid-thirties: the Unilever Combine.'[5] (Unilever had large chemical interests in Melanesia.)

It is not easy to establish just how many people Tom Harrisson persuaded to come and help him in Bolton (and in the holiday extension of Bolton 37 miles away, Blackpool) in the late thirties; or how long they stayed; or on what basis or bases. But it is clear that most helpers came for brief periods in return for minimal board and lodging (in the Mass-Observation headquarters at 85 Davenport Street, Bolton, and elsewhere); and that many were from

a background very different from the environment into which they came as observers. Although working-class people did help – for example, Harry Gordon (see below) – the majority of those who worked with Tom Harrisson were from the middle and upper classes:' . . . the Worktown end of this Mass-Observation turned from one person, somewhat adrift, into sometimes sixty observers at a time (especially during Oxford and Cambridge University vacations).'[6] Harrisson's temporary recruits included a number of well-known artists and writers: for example, Sir William Coldstream, William Empson, Julian Trevelyan, Michael Wickham – and Humphrey Spender.

Among all these people, the motivations for becoming involved in the Worktown project, the attractions of visiting Bolton and Blackpool, were mixed and varied considerably. They ranged from guilt born of a sense of privilege to the excitement (including for some, the aesthetic stimulation) of exploring unknown country; from the desire just to have a good time to an impulse to help make the world better by seeking out and disseminating the facts about other people's lives. And in a world made frightening by the rise of Fascism, some were looking for security and succour (even identity) among the strangers who made up the great majority of their compatriots.

Tom Harrisson sought on more than one occasion to distinguish between the attitudes to working-class people of himself (an ex-Harrovian) and those of George Orwell (an ex-Etonian) in the following way: 'It is difficult to remember (now) how in those far-off days, nearly everybody who was not born into the working-class regarded them as almost a

*When Mass-Observation became exclusively a market research organisation.
**See *Nella Last's War: A Mother's Diary, 1939-45,* edited by Richard Broad & Suzie Fleming, Falling Wall Press, 1981.

race apart. Even good books like George Orwell's *Road To Wigan Pier*, which really tried to get under the surface, started out (1937) from this underlying and sociologically miserable premise. The biggest thrill which this lately initiated "cannibal" [i.e Tom Harrisson himself] experienced [in Bolton] was finding it no more difficult to be accepted as an equal in a cotton mill, as a lorry driver or ice-cream man. The fact that one had an accent very acceptable on the BBC of those days in no way led to suspicion that one was "slumming" or "spying". It was only necessary to claim to have come from another dialect area a few miles away. (For one thing, no workers in their right senses ever supposed that anyone came to work in Worktown for any other reason than dire necessity!)'[7] To respect the main impulse represented here does not require one to respect all the implicit attitudes or believe all the statements. Compare Julian Trevelyan: 'I had also, through Mass-Observation, partly resolved for myself the problem that beset all my generation in the years before the war. We watched helplessly the growth of Fascism, extinguishing, as it seemed, one after another the liberties amongst which we had moved in our carefree way ten years before. The long-drawn-out struggle in Spain, the gradual shrinking of the republican territory where all our hopes lay – this seemed only symbolic of the betrayal of all that we cared for. Like so many of my friends I had flirted with Communism, and had been lured to meetings to hear Pollitt and Ted Bramley; as a Surrealist I had cooked Bomblets and marched in May Day processions; as a member of the Artists' International I had signed telegrams and badgered M.P.s. All this now seemed quite useless, and it was more by way of the enthusiasm of the Ashington miners for their paintings that I regained my faith in the more permanent values of our civilisation that had, so short a while ago, seemed to be running down to its own destruction.'[8] This is a much less artful piece of writing. Yet it was Tom Harrisson who 'had made contact with the Ashington group of miners who painted in their village in Northumberland'.[9] He certainly moved with ease from the homes of the industrial benefactors who contributed to Mass-Observation's funds – the Leverhulme family, the Barlow family – to the company of their lowest paid employees, in the pub or wherever. His was perhaps a unique ease: there was an arrogance about it, but it resulted in large measure from his openness to, his capacity for unjudging acceptance of, human variety.

Harrisson's allegiances were another matter. In a 'Postcript' to *Britain Revisited*, Charles Madge writes: 'Tom was more definitely and consistently unwilling to take sides politically than were I and some others of the small initial group at that time.'[10] But of course, this did not mean that he had no politics. His position had long been what he implied in 1975, when he wrote: 'The gap between leader and led, between published opinion and public opinion, between Westminster chatter and Lancashire talk built an invisible barrier, dangerous in our democracy.'[11] His was a familiar social-democratic position: the 'gap' for him was a matter of inadequate 'communication between the "two societies"',[12] a problem for the 'leaders'. His father had been a general, and later became managing director of the Argentinian railways. As an albeit irreverant and aberrant scion of the ruling class, at critical moments he readily took up a ruling class position. During the war, he was quite happy for Mass-Observation to be identified completely with the Government (Charles Madge broke with him on this issue): 'The more we did, the angrier the top people, the privileged few, became . . . even as late as 1940, when we were working for the Ministry of Information Lord Ritchie Calder [long before he became a lord – J.M.] caused an uproar by stating that we were virtually spies on our own society. There was a heated debate in Parliament on this theme of "Cooper's Snooper's", so named after the then Minister of Information the Right Hon. Duff Cooper (later Lord Norwich). Fortunately common sense prevailed: we won.'[13] It is characteristic that, at such a moment, Harrisson should pretend that 'we' were not the 'top people'. In 1970 he wrote, without a hint of self-questioning: ' . . . the panel of Mass-Observers, as well as the techniques for full-time investigation which we had considerably refined, proved of high value to governmental and other bodies';[14] and without a hint of irony: 'In the intervening years, Mass-Observation has used this basic study [*The Pub and the People*] in a number of so far unpublished investigations of other aspects of drinking and a long series of reports for clients interested in these problems (notably Guinness and Courage).'[15]

Tom Picton has written: 'In 1976, Tom Harrisson could write about the "mass" in *Living Through the Blitz* (Penguin, 1978): "They could contribute little more than to muddle through, obey the military law and maybe mutter a little." This suggests that the real job of winning the war was being done elsewhere. He was writing about an industrial working class without whose munitions *no* war would have been possible. The privations of war were not all that bad for the working class, he writes: "Putting up with discomfort, enduring economic uncertainty and periods of familiar distress, were built into pre-war 'working class' experience." The poor do not mind being poor, they are used to it.'[16] Picton's comments are entirely appropriate. They indicate one side of the most significant of Tom Harrisson's contradictions. On the one hand, he could be extraordinarily open to other people's lives (parts of *The Pub and the People** provide eloquent evidence of this); on the other hand, his political allegiances induced such distorted vision.

A number of Tom Harrisson's strengths were also his weaknesses: for example, his capacity to generate plans and proposals and to enthuse other people with them, his obsession with detail, his willingness to rush off in any direction that seemed to offer the realisation of an interesting half-idea. Since he was such a key figure, it seems certain that, even without the intervention of the war, Mass-Observation would have achieved much less than it promised. Yet the Archive itself is there, a sort of unique achievement in itself, exemplified at its best by Humphrey Spender's photographs. Taken at Tom Harrisson's request, but without anything except the vaguest of plans for their possible use, they remained virtually unknown and unused during four decades. As Spender says on page 21, for Harrisson, 'in a sense, the main thing was that they were there'.

---

*This was mainly the work of John Sommerfield, but was heavily influenced by Harrisson.

Spender in Worktown

Because of his Worktown photography, and similar work done elsewhere, Humphrey Spender is usually referred to as a 'documentary photographer', both within a specifically British movement of 'documentary photography' (and 'documentary film') in the thirties and forties, and within a wider context, in which German 'documentary' influences are mapped and American 'documentary' similarities suggested. In other words, the term is used a lot, usually as though it were self-explanatory. 'Documentary' seems to imply that photographs so called have documented reality in such a way that the 'evidence' they contain can be 'read' from them in a simple way. Is this so?

While most of the artists invited to Bolton were intended, it appears, to provide a subjective response to Worktown; Humphrey Spender's task, as photographer, was posed as akin to that of the great majority of helpers on the Worktown project, who came to be surreptitious observers, recording a mass of detail – in principle, about anything to do with life in Bolton and Blackpool. Spender himself says, on page 23, that his prime function was to 'provide information'. So concerned was Tom Harrisson to have pictures of people uninfluenced in their behaviour and appearance by the presence of a camera, that he was against taking photographs of domestic interiors; and Spender went along with this – despite the fact that, earlier in the thirties, he had painstakingly and successfully photographed a Stepney family in their home. Even so, while most of the photographs in this book are by an 'unobserved observer', a significant number are not: for example, the young woman holding a bobbin on page 47, the bathing of the baby on page 54, and the bowlers on pages 64 and 65. Yet their quality is at one with other photographs in the book taken without their subject's knowledge. So a second question is, why should this be?

Answering the first question helps to answer the second. In many of the Worktown photographs, there is much that can be taken readily from them. An obvious example is the picture of Blackpool beach on page 115, where, among other things, everybody's clothing is immediately striking. The interest of such data makes it puzzling that, given his obsession with the collection of data of all kinds, Tom Harrisson was so concerned to have 'candid' photographs. (The information about clothing in the beach scene would have been no different if some of the holiday-makers had been posed.) Posed pictures *can* carry genuine information; unposed pictures *can* be misleading. In the posed photograph of the bathing of the baby, it is, ironically, 'unposed' elements that are misleading – in particular, the fireplace. It is impossible to 'read' this photograph correctly unaided, except by guesswork. One needs the sort of gloss provided in the note to page 54. The photograph of the group in front of the Post Office on page 28 provides another example. Both Humphrey Spender and I had assumed that these were middle-class women, until Harry Gordon suggested otherwise. Part of the answer to the first question, then, is that these 'documentary' photographs can easily be 'read' for information, but many of them can easily be read wrongly. They require other information to complement them.

The reader may ask why, therefore, there is not a lot more information alongside the photographs. The reason is that there was no possibility that this book could be, in any sense, comprehensive. Although Spender took a great many photographs, altogether – as he emphasises on page 20 – they constitute nothing like a comprehensive view of Bolton and Blackpool. A selection of a hundred or so, as here, from the six to seven hundred possibles makes for an even greater arbitrariness. At the same time, the task of collecting and organising a great deal more information to go with them would be a major research enterprise. The Notes and the bits of information given later in this Introduction are intended to be pointers, and a reminder that the photographs themselves are only pointers, in the reconstruction of a piece of the past. And so it seemed better to let the photographs come before the reader only minimally captioned: first, in order to avoid an implicit claim to comprehensiveness (a dense collage of images and text can give a convincing *imitation* of comprehensiveness); and secondly, to let the quality of the photographs communicate directly, in an uncluttered way, qualified only subsequently by reference to the Notes. This brings us back to the earlier two questions.

'Reading' Humphrey Spender's photographs in a second sense, that of taking their quality and responding to the photographer in them, seems not to be a matter for general agreement. In front of me as I write is a copy of the *Guardian* announcing an exhibition at the Arnolfini Gallery in Bristol. Spender's pictures of Jarrow hunger marchers are – almost incredibly – described as 'gloomy', when (I would have thought) it is difficult to deny that they are generally buoyant in feeling. Either the writer hadn't seen them but assumed they were gloomy because that is the received view of the thirties, or didn't actually see what was in front of him or her for the same reason.

A comparable example is the remark by Stephen McClarence in *Photographers* about the Worktown photographs: 'You can almost see Spender's look of perplexed revulsion reflected in the camera lens.'[21] This occurs in an article that is in many respects well done, and which contains material from an interview with Spender in which he describes the ways in which he found Bolton 'depressing', and the job he was doing, unpleasant. I can only think that McClarence has interpreted this as meaning recoil from the people there, and then projected this on to the photographs. I can find no recoil from the people in Bolton and Blackpool in Humphrey Spender's photographs: quite the reverse. Nor do I see the 'detachment' that some people profess to see in his work. Perhaps they have assumed it because of Mass-Observation's typical procedures.

The Worktown photographs convey, to me, a rare feeling of equality between photographer and subject. Spender may have 'reacted to stereotype' on occasions, as he says on page 16, but a strong discipline derived from a natural tact and empathy, together with a lot of hard self-training, prevented this from entering the photographs. And where they are gloomy, there is no imposed gloom. Moreover, the technical limitations of Spender's equipment and film meant that, as often as possible, he photographed people at moments of stillness; which in turn meant that he was often an onlooker photographing onlookers. This can communicate an overall feeling which, at a glance, is confusable with a lack of engagement – a detachment – on the part of the photographer; but which is actually its opposite.

The experience of looking again and again at these photographs over a period of nearly two years has, for me, had the effect of dissolving a surprising amount of what – of course – they carry from another society, another time and place. So much so that I have been taken aback when people new to them have sometimes remarked on how different people looked then.

Commenting on a Bill Brandt photograph in the exhibition, *The Real Thing: An anthology of British photography 1840-1950* at the Hayward Gallery, Caroline Tisdall wrote: 'Myths are still at work in Bill Brandt's portrait of a miner at home and eating. It all rings true, the detail of the room, the unceremonious approach. There's just one fatal fault in the realism: in his effort to get the picture of the miner at home, Brandt has skipped the one fact that gives the lie – a miner would never sit down to his meal without scrubbing off first.'[22] There seems to have been no possibility of such a thing happening in Humphrey Spender's work for Mass-Observation. What creates the consistency between his posed photographs and those taken as an unobserved observer is the fact that in neither does he impose himself. He engages with his subjects, and expresses his own sensibility, but not at their expense. Indeed, that is at the core of his sensibility.

Bolton

In 1937, the population was about 170,400, and reckoned to be decreasing at the rate of about 1,000 a year. The number of people in full-time employment was officially 96,566 (of whom 35,976 were women). Almost exactly a third worked in the cotton industry. Sixty per cent of all school-leavers went into cotton. The number of registered unemployed was 10,758 – i.e. 11% of the 'working population' as against 6.4% in London and the South-East, and a national average of 10.8%. The death-rate was 14.2 per 1,000. This was significantly high: after correction for age distribution differences between Bolton and the rest of the United Kingdom, it was 25% higher than the national average. This was probably due largely to tuberculosis associated with the cotton industry — overwhelmingly the cause of death in adults of 'working age'. (These statistics come not from the Mass-Observation Archive, but from the Report of Bolton's Medical Officer of Health for 1937, and from the Central Office of Information.)

Many of the buildings pictured in this book have been demolished, to make way for new houses, new shops, new roads and new industry – or proposed new houses, new shops, new roads and new industry. With the gradual collapse of the cotton industry, many mills have been closed or converted to new uses. (The mill that the women are leaving after work on page 50 now has 'Flash Mills Kitchen D.I.Y. Centre' on its arch, with a notice to one side saying 'Bombay Restaurant'.) Travelling around Bolton, you continually come upon bits of Humphrey Spender's photographs; and occasionally, more than just bits. The corner where the boys are running on page 42 is still clearly recognisable (though the mill behind is not a mill now). But housewives no longer infuriate coalmen of a Monday morning in Back Todd Street (pages 41, 52 and 53); and the view from what is left of Merehall Park (page 74) has been transformed. The Mass-Observation headquarters in Bolton, 85 Davenport Street – in a terrace that, along with many other terraces, huddled among mills less than half a mile from the town centre – was demolished in 1981. Later in the year, you could still find what might have been some of its rubble, on the edge of a wasteland now designated for major roadways, council housing and other building.

The Photographs, the Notes and Further Reading

All the selected photographs were printed especially for this book – almost all of them by Humphrey Spender himself, and the remainder by Jan Siegieda under Spender's direction. All have been printed without cropping. This, together with the fact that some of the negatives have deteriorated or been damaged over the years, accounts for the variations in border, and for the occasional appearance of sprocket marks.

Harry Gordon's comments in the Notes were recorded in 1981. Now aged 76, and still living in Bolton, he was an unemployed fitter when he helped Tom Harrisson in 1937. Very little of the work done in the Worktown project has been published. The only book that arose directly from the project (and the one chiefly quoted in the Notes) is *The Pub and the People*; the other book quoted in the Notes, *Britain Revisited*, was written as a result of Tom Harrisson revisiting Bolton and Blackpool in 1960, and contains material from the late thirties for purposes of comparison. (See the full references below.)

Articles about Humphrey Spender and Mass-Observation can be found in the catalogue to the exhibition, *Worktown: Photographs of Bolton and Blackpool Taken for Mass-Observation 1937/38*, University of Sussex, 1977; and in *Camerawork* No. 11. For a useful and interesting account of the origins and context of Mass-Observation, and of its development, see Tom Jeffery, *Mass-Observation: A Short History*, Centre for Contemporary Cultural Studies Occasional Paper SP No. 55, University of Birmingham, 1978. These three publications together provide a wide range of suggestions for further reading; and all three are in print (January 1982), and available from the Mass-Observation Archive, University of Sussex, Falmer, Brighton.

Jeremy Mulford

References

1 Charles Madge & Tom Harrisson, *Mass-Observation*, London, Muller, 1937, p. 10. 2 Quoted in Tom Harrisson, 'The Mass-Observation Archive at Sussex University', *Aslib Proceedings*, August 1971, p.398. 3 Tom Harrisson, *Britain Revisited*, London, Gollancz, 1961, p.25. 4 Ibid., p. 26. 5 Ibid., p.25. 6 Ibid., p. 26. 7 Tom Harrisson, Preface to the 1970 reprint (by Seven Dials Press, Welwyn Garden City) of Mass-Observation, *The Pub and the People: A Worktown Study*, London, Gollancz, 1943, p.6. 8 Julian Trevelyan, *Indigo Days*, London, MacGibbon & Kee, 1957, p. 102. 9 Ibid., p. 92 10 *Britain Revisited*, p. 277. 11 *Britain in the 30s* (published in a limited edition of 100 copies with an Introduction and Commentary by Tom Harrisson), London, Lion and Unicorn Press, Royal College of Art, 1975 (pages unnumbered). 12 Ibid. 13 Ibid. 14 1970 Preface to *The Pub and the People*, p.5. 15 Ibid., p.8. 16 Tom Picton, 'A very public espionage', *Camerawork* No. 11, p.2. 17 *Mass-Observation*, p.47. 18 *Aslib Proceedings*, August 1971, p. 401. 19 *Indigo Days*, p.84. 20 'Briefing', *Guardian*, 16 December 1981. 21 Stephen McClarence, 'The Quiet Observer: An Interview with Humphrey Spender', *Photographers*, No. 4, Aug-Oct 1979, p.5. 22 *Guardian*, 19 March 1975.

Interview with Humphrey Spender*

The Making of a Photographer

Humphrey Spender was born in 1910. He came from what he describes as 'a privileged background of frequently changing nannies and governesses and two devoted servants'. His father, Harold Spender, was a well-known journalist and promoter of Liberal and philanthropic causes. His mother became an invalid as a result of having four children in too rapid succession. Both his parents died before he was sixteen. He was educated at small private schools in Worthing and Hampstead; and then went to the public school, Gresham's School in Norfolk, where he was a younger contemporary of the poet, W.H. Auden.

JM : When was the first time you ever used a camera?

HS : I was about nine. An uncle sent me a box camera from Switzerland. I was so fascinated by it as an object — its finish, its shine, the jewel-like appearance of the viewfinder and lens, the feel of the shutter mechanism, the loading mechanism, even the smell of its black interior — that I hardly thought of its purpose.

At the time, my elder brother, Michael, was mad about photographing steam engines and railways. I adored him, and I used to follow him about, helping him. He was about four years older than me, and just very clever. It was mainly he who taught me about the technique of photography. He was an impatient person, and couldn't tolerate people failing and mucking around, so I was slightly panicky all the time about doing the wrong thing; but he was a very good instructor. His camera used glass plates, and we did all the processing in the attic bathroom of the house in Hampstead where we lived. Of course, that

*Edited transcript of a series of interviews by Jeremy Mulford during 1981.

kind of processing is very much out of date now, but the basic principles were to be understood from that activity.

JM : What other cameras did you have when you were young?

HS : All kinds of names crop up, mostly German — Voigtlaender, Agfa, Zeiss, Rolleiflex, and the Kodak Retina, one of the first popular 35mm cameras and — like the Voigtlaender — a bellows camera. Michael believed that good lenses were made only in Germany, and it was he who persuaded me to buy the very expensive Leitz Leica when I was about eighteen, probably the 1925 model. Once again I was spellbound by a camera as object, as wonderful precision machinery. I still have it.

JM : What sort of photographs were you taking in the late twenties?

HS : Oh, pretty boring — what would nowadays be called 'tourist photographs'. When I was in Freiburg, for instance, one of the family came out and we did a trip round the Black Forest: I simply took pretty architecture, pretty Baroque churches, the normal idea of the picturesque. Very boring they were.

Humphrey Spender's maternal grandfather was German, and his grandmother — by now his guardian — had thought it appropriate for him to go to Freiburg University for a year, to learn the language and study art history in the fashionable way. After a year, he returned to London to become an architectural student.

JM : Why did you choose to study architecture?

HS : I didn't. My hyperactive grandmother was extremely worried about all our occupations and futures, and I've always imagined a conversation that went something like this: 'Humphrey's quite good at drawing, he's not bad at mathematics — whatever do you think is a good thing for him to do? I mean, we don't count painting as work, as a way of

making your living.' 'What about architecture?' said someone, probably some uncle or other. And I was suddenly told it would be a good idea if I went to the Architectural Association School of Architecture. So this was arranged.

JM : Was photography your main interest?

HS : No, not by any means. It was a complementary activity. I liked the limitations imposed by the processes, as opposed to the wide range of decision-making involved in painting, and also in architecture. At the same time, the moment you get involved in making your own photographic prints, then all kinds of things happen. You see all kinds of possibilities, which have failed to emerge in commercial printing. There's absolutely no doubt that the most important part of producing a good photograph is in making the print. I realised that very early on; and because of my elder brother, I was always striving to produce the perfect print. Also, once I possessed an enlarger, I started all kinds of tricks with it, which fascinated me for their own sake. But my main interest was painting, which I started doing at the age of six. Since then I have always struggled with it. I think if anybody had asked me when I was eighteen or nineteen, 'What would you most like to be good at?', I would have said, 'Painting.' But looking back on it, I now think I didn't work hard enough. There were terrible temptations just to travel and fritter time.

JM : Did you have any formal training in drawing or painting?

HS : No, except what was given at architectural training, which overall was quite tough. Tough but extremely bad, very reactionary. It harked back to *appearance*, to the Beaux-Arts schools of architecture, with their preoccupation with classical architecture: you drew a central axis and then draped things in mirror image around that central axis. A few of us started a movement that rebelled against this. We were extremely unpleasant to our tutors —

much more rude than any of my own students has ever been to me. Of course, we raved about Le Corbusier, Gropius, the Bauhaus, Mies van der Rohe; and there were other cult figures, whose names have since vanished, that were very important in what we thought of as modern architecture in those days. Our lines of thought were probably rather superficial; but it was the *beginnings* of a feeling that architecture should be much more about people's lives than about pomposity and the planning of grand vistas and public buildings. What was anathema to us was the kind of thing being perpetrated in New Delhi by Herbert Baker and Lutyens — grandiose public monuments, laid out with great avenues and vistas. We raked up all the scandals we could about them. We were full of contempt for what was going on generally in architecture. I think we were just *for* avant-garde architecture, for simplification. 'Functionalism' was one of the great words, you see.

JM : Which people were influencing you most?

HS : Michael had ceased to be a god when I was about fourteen. To a certain extent my other brother, Stephen, had replaced him, and friends of his such as Christopher Isherwood and Wystan Auden were awe-inspiring models. Even more influential was my fellow student, Bill Edmiston. He had precocious talents in many directions, acting, singing, designing, drawing, fashion. You could really describe my life as being that of a member of the intelligentsia. My own accusation against myself, looking back now, would be that I was very dilletante. My finger was in a lot of pies. I was interested in all creative work — painting, photography, films, music — just a dilettante really, wasting an awful lot of time, but trying myself to be a painter. As a painter, very much influenced by the brothers Nash (Paul was also a photographic influence) — and others whose names will mean little or nothing now, like Mark Gertler (though, actually, he is now being revived) and Ethelbert White: probably nobody has ever heard of Ethelbert White, but he was a very influential painter in those days. And, of course, it was the Picasso era and, shamefully late, we were beginning to be rocked by his work, and by that of Braque and Matisse.

In photography, I bought journals with titles like 'Modern Photography' and 'Photographs of the Year'; and without any particular attachment to names, I would find my favourite photographs. There was one kind of photograph in which the Japanese seemed to specialise, and which intrigued me — typical would be a close-up of a flower with raindrops, very sharply focussed, disposing themselves in the way that raindrops do on petals, like water on a duck's back. In producing that sort of photograph myself, I was aiming at something which I now consider generally boring, just the 'beautiful photograph'.

One name that stands out was Hans Casparius, who was a stills photographer for German films. His work involved the heavy use of filters to bring out very intensely the blue of the sky, as a dark tone against which shone flesh and stone and leaf. There was a German magazine called *Querschnitt [Cross-Section]*, which my brother and I got imported, and Casparius was often featured in it. He influenced me a lot. I remember even buying a red filter, which made skies absolutely black. To a certain extent I'm still fascinated by very dark, dramatic skies. Other names I remember were Hoyningen-Huené, Man Ray, Moholy-Nagy and Lucia Moholy (who was a friend of my grandmother's). And there was Cecil Beaton, though we rather hooted at him. His was a name that then represented a kind of smart-set photography; but to do him justice, he turns out, in retrospect, to have been a better photographer than we then thought.

Many of the photographers whose work I admired I didn't particularly register at the time. For example, when I first read a few years ago that I'd been influenced by the Hungarian, André Kertesz, I hadn't a clue who Kertesz was. But when I looked in books containing some of his photographs, I realised I had in fact looked at his work in the past and liked it enormously, without identifying or remembering his name. His photographs were very straight, sharp definition, record — a kind of photography that recorded people and events, not just pretty patterns or accidental effects of light.

JM : And Cartier-Bresson?

HS : I can't honestly remember when I first heard of

Cartier-Bresson, but it seems to me that from a very early time I have been enthusiastic about his work.

JM : What about moving pictures?

HS : Many of the marvellous films we saw at the weekly showings of the Film Society in London were powerful visual influences — such films as Eisenstein's *Battleship Potemkin*, Lang's *Metropolis*, Kauffmann's *Spring*, Pabst's *The White Hell of Piz Palu* (Hans Casparius was the stills photographer for that). And there was one film in particular, which — like Kertesz — I'd quite forgotten, and which I was reminded of only recently, Ruttman's *Berlin: the Symphony of a Great City*. This was an early documentary produced with hidden cameras in 1928, and certainly had a formative influence on me.

JM : So when did you start to get bored with the sort of 'beautiful photograph' that you were speaking about earlier?

HS : Well, what happens after you've taken a lot of photographs? You go on accumulating them, but what do you do with them? Either you lose interest in them and leave them in drawers, or you put them in albums, and gradually you acquire more and more of those. So you become more selective, and throw a lot out. For me, it was a matter partly of interpreting the reactions of my friends, who were saying, 'Oh yes, that's very nice,' and clearly suppressing a yawn. Also, you ask yourself, how do *you* react if somebody says, 'Oh, I must show you the pictures I took the last time I was in India'? My friends always found more interesting the photographs that were of people, friends and relations: and I myself always found the same about other people's photographs. I think I must suddenly have realised that you can interpret photographs of people in so many different, so many *more* ways. The development of a growing person, for instance — one year's photograph being different from the previous one, the next year's showing advance, showing growth, and so on. Moreover, this may be thinking with hindsight, but I think I was always particularly interested in the unexpected photograph, when people were taken without their knowing.

JM : Given your background, what was your view of society generally, what were your political views, from the beginning of the thirties onwards?

HS : There was much that horrified me: slums, the terrible standard of living of many people, unemployment. One of my great friends was a probation officer, a woman called Clémence Paine, who worked for a very well-known magistrate called Basil Henriques. He sat in the juvenile courts, and was dealing with East End children — Stepney, Mile End, the Docks, the Isle of Dogs — and she was always telling me horrific stories about the reasons why these children were committing petty crimes. Incidentally, these crimes were usually not nearly so bad as those often committed now; but many children were being brought into court. Both Basil Henriques and the probation officers treated the children very humanely. Arising from this, my friend asked me to help her publicise the conditions in Stepney, and I took a whole set of photographs of Stepney slums, which have since acquired a lot of sociological interest. But I have to admit to being only on the fringe of political activity. If I was asked to participate, as for instance when the magazine *Left Review*, which was a politically militant journal, asked me to photograph the Hunger Marchers, I willingly did so, feeling that I ought to do something.

An important experience was that of photographing (again for *Left Review*, I think) a Mosley meeting of British Fascists in the Albert Hall, where actual physical threats by blackshirted Fascist thugs brought home the need to take seriously what was happening in Germany. I think my friends and I were very aware of the menace of Hitler vis-à-vis the Jews (my family is part-Jewish), although quite a lot of people were wishfully thinking that everything was OK. Politically, if I had been asked then to describe my attachment, I would have said I was left. I was in sympathy rather naively with an idealised version of Communism. I did not align myself to the extent that Stephen did, to the point of actually joining the Party; but I was certainly sympathetic. Our family background was strongly Liberal — my father had stood as a Liberal candidate for Parliament — so that's where my sympathies lay: Liberalism and the left.

JM : What effect did the Spanish Civil War have on you?

HS : The German involvement, the bombing of Guernica in 1937, together with reading books from the Left Book Club which disclosed the machinations of the armament manufacturers — these influenced me greatly. Ever since then my general line of thought has been to do with the horrors of arms manufacture, with the fact that many, many people have been made wealthy by selling death, so to speak. I feel it very strongly at the moment, that this is what Mrs. Thatcher has been up to in the Middle East [spring 1981], that she has simply been selling death.

It was Left Book Club books that confirmed my own political attachment. Yet now I feel ashamed that I wasn't much more committed, actively, to furthering the causes that I respected. I was militant to the extent that I did what I was asked, as for instance with the Stepney photographs when I was an architectural student; but I failed to take enough initiative myself.

JM : How difficult was it for you to make a living yourself in the thirties?

HS : I emerged from the Architectural Association in 1934, when there was perhaps the biggest industrial slump in history; and whereas we were supposed to do six months in an architect's office in order to get our qualification, it was so difficult to get work that this was written out of the conditions. So I got my Diploma and did, in fact, get work with a Polish refugee. (Already, in 1934, there were Germans and Austrians and Poles who were leaving their countries and coming here.) This man was doing interiors for very grand houses, in places like Berkeley Square, and he was doing them up with everything I disliked, such as gilded reproduction furniture. And the first thing he gave me to do was the perspective drawing for an interior in Berkeley Square. My drawing was looking through the room on to windows that opened down to the floor, out on to a balcony; so I made them open and concentrated most of my effort on the scene outside, into which I put a lamppost and a dog peeing. And this man — his name was Landauer — said, 'Mr. Spender, I think you're hardly suited to this kind of work.' That job lasted three days. There may have been one other job, which lasted a very short time, but

then I decided, with my friend Bill Edmiston, to start a photographic studio.

We got a sequence of rooms in the Strand in central London for six pounds a week, which was cheap even for those days, and turned them into a studio. We already had equipment, of course, but we bought more: a large format reflex camera, probably secondhand; a marvellous tripod, I remember; various items of darkroom equipment, good enlargers; a lot of material for backgrounds, stuff that we thought was very modern — silver paper and gauze — with spotlights. We took any work we could get hold of, through personal contacts, and one job led to another. We had contacts with the *Architectural Review*; and Eddy — Bill Edmiston — had contacts in the fashion world, and we worked for *Harper's Bazaar*, *Vogue* and other magazines. Eddy was more or less in charge of the fashion stuff, because I didn't know a lot about it, and I was more or less in charge of the straight architectural photography, which gave me a chance to exploit my liking for dark skies and cloud effects. We worked together on some covers for the *Architectural Review* which showed strong surrealist influences. We also did a lot of incredibly boring advertising photography — cold cream jars, things like that — anything we could get.

This went on and we were doing fairly well — I think we were quite good — until one day the phone rang and it was the *Daily Mirror*. One of the directors, Guy Bartholomew, had come up with an idea for introducing a touch of 'Art' into the *Mirror*: 'Lensman' was to be the pseudonym for a roving photographer taking 'artistic' photographs all over the country. For some unexplained reason they were inviting one of us to do the job. Bill Edmiston didn't want it, so I took it on, and the partnership with him gradually died.

Unfortunately, Lensman was under the control of the resident art editor, H. Rider-Rider. From the moment he set eyes on me he absolutely loathed me, which I realised straight away. I was everything he disliked — a sort of posh-speaking upstart, I suppose he would have said — so he tried to put me down from the word go. I started on the lines that Bartholomew had envisaged, cruising around the country in a car. But what the art editor thought was art was not what I thought was art, and I soon realised that I was not really able to provide what he wanted. For a while, though, fairly happily I played his hand, and photographed a range of picturesque English villages, bits of countryside. Occasionally, he would say things like, 'If you're at a loss, then find a pretty girl, put her on a horse, take her on the downs, clouds in the sky, hair blowing in the wind' — that kind of photograph, which I could do fairly well. There was one occasion, in Wales, when it was pouring with rain. I had to telephone the art editor to see if there was anything special he wanted me to do; and he said, 'Oh well, it's raining, you can't photograph out of doors. Find an old lady, some national costume, a spinning wheel; set her down in a homely country cottage, and take that. Use your imagination, man.'

I didn't say much about that sort of thing at the time, but obviously I didn't like it. And gradually the art editor put me down, and other photographers became Lensman also. In particular, Harry Greenwell, who was a very good photographer, and who became in the end more important as Lensman than I was. My final burst as Lensman was to be sent to Morocco. It all happened very suddenly, and I discovered afterwards it was because the *Daily Mirror* had been involved in a libel action with an air transport firm, who had lost, owing the *Mirror* something like £500 — the equivalent of, say, £4,000 today. They were paying off the money in flights, and one of those flights was mine to Morocco. The pilot was a bewildering drunk, who flew me in a most hazardous and terrifying way, in a two-seater Puss Moth, taking five days to reach Tangiers. That was how the trip came about, but it produced a lot of good pictures, of which they used twelve or thirteen.

Soon after that I was sacked, because I refused to go and take a comic photograph of Edith Sitwell wearing a fruit-laden hat the day after I had met her with my brother. The art editor's reaction was, 'Orders is orders. If I tell you to go and photograph your brother in a *pool of blood*, you will do so.' Bartholomew had me up to his office and said, 'Obviously, you're fighting this man, and therefore the job is unsympathetic. Take three times your salary

for three months and stay away.' That seemed to me a terrific arrangement, so I did just that. My salary had been £9 per week, so I got £27 a week for doing nothing for three months. I think I went to Austria. I love travelling, and all this time I'd been taking every opportunity to go to places like Venice, Innsbruck, Berlin, just travelling. As a family, because of our parents having died when we were young, we had independent means to the point where, although we had to work, we could afford to take time off for holidays.

My memory for these things is fairly useless, but I think it was soon after leaving the *Mirror* that I was asked to join the original team of photographers working for *Picture Post*, which was first published towards the end of 1938. So I began working alongside Felix Man, Bert Hardy, Clark Hutton and Thurston Hopkins. I think the assistant editor, Tom Hopkinson (later the editor), may well have seen the Stepney photographs, the Hunger March photographs, and perhaps some of the Mass-Observation photographs which I started taking in 1937: somehow he knew I was using a 35mm camera. And *Picture Post* was in the vanguard of illustrated magazines using miniature cameras in this country.

As Lensman, I had always battled to use a 35mm camera — certainly I used one in Morocco, for example — but the *Daily Mirror*, like other newspapers, very strongly resisted miniature cameras. The main reason was that the small size of the negatives didn't allow any retouching in the darkroom. I don't know to what extent this goes on now, but newspaper photography then depended an awful lot on touching up the negatives, particularly the girly pictures.

JM : So you became involved in a new kind of journalism?

HS : New for this country, yes. *Picture Post* was based on the current German illustrated papers, like *Frankfurte Illustrierte* and *Münchene Illustrierte*, in which there were feature stories that were several pages long, with more photographs than text. Stefan Lorant, who as a Jewish editor had in fact been imprisoned by Hitler in Munich, came over from Germany with this idea, and Edward Hulton persuaded that this was something that could suc-

ceed here. *Picture Post* was intended for a popular readership, and Hulton was certainly out to make profit. But the writers and photographers, who tended to be radically inclined, were allowed much more scope to put their own view of things. (Hulton recognised that this was one way to sell papers.) For myself, the best example of the difference between working for *Picture Post* and working for the *Mirror* is provided by the fact that I was sent to Tyneside by both papers. For the *Mirror*, I'd been expected to make the industrial scene picturesque, including unemployment; whereas for *Picture Post* we were able to produce a feature of realism so harsh that we evoked a strong complaint from the mayor.

JM : How long did you work for *Picture Post*?

HS : Until I was called up in 1941.

Humphrey Spender first trained for tanks in the Royal Army Service Corps on Salisbury Plain. Basic training as a trooper 'was suddenly and inexplicably interrupted by total discharge. Then I had a puzzled period of official non-existence which was ended when I sent a telegram to the War Office: their answer revealed that they'd forgotten their intention to use me as an Official Photographer, with a direct commission (second lieutenant) in the General List. It was just chance that put me in a batch of officer photographers, as opposed to non-commissioned officer photographers (like Bert Hardy). Immediately, I was involved in a 'them and us' set-up, having to cope with the same kind of class-conscious embarrassments that I'd had to face in working for Mass-Observation in Bolton. Except for the occasional episode that brought fear followed by hospitalisation — an abortive commando raid that ended in a shower of bombs and shells, a crash in a glider on Salisbury Plain with a group of equally frightened Members of Parliament — my official photographic work was routine. In the archives of the Imperial War Museum, there is some fairly unspectacular work done while tagging along behind brass hats who occasionally included the King: various jobs I'd done for Picture Post *during the first eighteen months of the war were much more like active service — for example, life on a mine-sweeper, life on a destroyer chasing submarines, wartime* coastguards, and so on.' In 1944, because of the worsening fatal illness of his first wife Margaret, he was transferred into photo-interpretation, working exclusively in England. His work included searching out VI rocket sites and making maps with T.I.S. (Theatre Intelligence Service) for the Normandy invasion.

Around the end of the war, Humphrey Spender suffered 'a period of rather stunned inactivity' after first his friend Bill Edmiston had been killed on active service, then his brother Michael had been killed in an air crash, and finally his wife had died after being ill and in considerable pain throughout the war. However, 'the boredom of waiting for demob' activated him into entering a competition for textile design, one of whose judges was Henry Moore. He won, and gradually there developed a career of designing alongside painting and renewed but sporadic photographic work for Picture Post. In the forties and fifties, he had frequent one-man shows of his paintings, and received many commissions for textiles, carpets, mural paintings and mosaics (including a mural in the Television Pavilion built for the Festival of Britain in 1951). After 1953, he gave up professional photography completely. In 1956, a crisis in the teaching policy of the Textile School at the Royal College of Art led to an invitation to be a part-time tutor, 'in order to counteract a too strong commercial trend in the School'. He accepted, and continued in this capacity until 1975. During that period and since, he has had teaching assignments at many other colleges of art.

Humphrey Spender adopted a son with his first wife; and has another son by his second wife — the actress and writer, Pauline Spender — whom he married in 1948.

'Worktown'

It was during 1937 and 1938, mainly while he was still working for the Daily Mirror, that Humphrey Spender took photographs for Mass-Observation. This unpaid work was part of the survey of Bolton ('Worktown'), together with the holiday resort of Blackpool, initiated and supervised by Mass-Observation's co-founder, Tom Harrisson. (For more about Mass-Observation and the Worktown survey, see the Introduction above.)

JM : How did you get involved with Mass-Observation?

HS : Tom Harrisson must have seen the photographs published in Left Review. Also, he knew my brother Michael (they had been on a scientific expedition together to the Great Barrier Reef), and he may well have seen the Stepney photographs at our house. He may even have known that I had applied (unsuccessfully) to be a stills photographer with John Grierson's documentary film unit.

Really, there were two sorts of reason why I accepted Tom's invitation to become involved in the Worktown project. On the one hand, I thought what he was proposing would be useful. He was an anthropologist, proposing to study human behaviour in our own country; and without doubt at that time I felt that knowing more about human behaviour could only improve the general quality of life. I was in sympathy with a very strong line of his, that the mass media misrepresented working-class life and public opinion generally. If the papers came out with headlines declaring that the whole nation was indignant at something or other, he would say the whole nation simply hadn't noticed that whatever it was had happened, so how could they be indignant about it? — and I was inclined to agree with him. On the other hand, Tom himself was a very magnetic personality. For me the most important thing about him was perhaps his ability to make people laugh. He succeeded in making me laugh quite uncontrollably, so that sometimes I was lying around on the floor just laughing. Laughter was a very important factor in our relationship. Although many people sooner or later came to loathe him, particularly women, he did have an inspiring quality that convinced you he was involved in very valuable work.

JM : What directions did he give you as a photographer? How did you come to choose some subjects and not others?

HS : There were never any written directives. Once he had persuaded you to come and live in the scruffy M-O headquarters in 85 Davenport Street, Bolton, there was a daily session which usually took the form of Tom seizing about half a dozen national newspapers, reading the headlines, getting us laughing and interested, and quite on the spur of the moment, impulsively, hitting on a theme that he thought would be productive. For instance, how people hold their hands, the number of sugar lumps that people pop into their mouths in restaurants, how much people stole things like teaspoons in restaurants, matches, bits of paper. Anything. Every day started with a kind of lead, and then you were working on your own, and one thing led to another.

Overall there was a general brief to produce information about people's behaviour in all kinds of situation — bus queues, football crowds, people in restaurants, people in pubs, people in church, people walking about the streets, people talking to each other, people not talking to each other, what they were wearing, whether they wore hats, what they wore on their feet — the list was endless, and a great mixture. Tom loaded me with objectives, too many objectives, and it was simply up to me. He badgered me, he nagged me for the results — 'Have you done total immersion? Have you done a christening? Have you done a holy communion?' — so I was never at a loss for something to do.

JM : But how would you characterise what you were setting out to do with the Mass-Observation photography?

HS : I think I do remember consciously having the thought that Tom Harrisson might wish to prove various things, but I was not going to get involved in that. I was aware that he was being attacked, very frequently, for trying to manipulate his observations, so I was taking great pains not to produce photographs merely as illustrations to theories of my own or theories Tom Harrisson had. I had quite a lot of sympathy with his critics. In fact, I remember having the thought that, in a way, it would almost be more interesting to disprove what he believed, to prove that he was wrong sometimes, that he was a bad scientist. You see, my brother Michael, who was a very strict orthodox scientist, thought of Tom merely as a sensational journalist who was manipulating facts. So I certainly made a very conscious effort to allow things to speak for themselves, and not to impose any kind of theory.

I suppose with a touch of hindsight I can say I was out to expose truths — though from the small amount of work I was able to do, the amount of time I was able to give it, any generalisations were going to have to be based on rather sparse evidence. Which, of course, is a very unsafe thing to do, and for which we — the whole Mass-Observation movement — have been criticised generally.

JM : In what ways did Tom Harrisson manipulate facts to suit his preconceptions?

HS : I think Tom, having worked a lot in remote parts of the world, was perhaps too anxious to find parallels in the life of this country. And so, having observed ritualistic dancing, and the masks, the costumes and other art connected with it, he would constantly be on the lookout for the same sort of thing in Bolton. For example, at every possible opportunity the children used to put on paper hats and dance about: these were quite innocent, childish affairs, but Tom was inclined to put rather mysterious interpretations on them. He had a tendency to wish things on to events in that way.

JM : What was your own response to Bolton?

HS : To be slightly frightened. I felt very much a foreigner. That depended on accent, and the types of clothes you were wearing, and the fact that in any strange town you've got to find your way about. I've got no sense of direction and was always getting lost: quite often, if I asked for directions, it was difficult to understand what people were saying. And the whole landscape, the townscape, was severe and made me apprehensive. There was a particular kind of dark red brick up there, a particular dark green to the grass, from the pollution; and the height of the factory chimneys, with smoke belching from them — these were alarming. In general, the experience was alarming — and depressing, because of the evident poverty, or at least the lack of anything that could be called luxury. People tended to look preoccupied, if not actually unhappy — though when you were in a pub, there was a kind of community feeling, the feeling of a lot of people who knew each other, and who were happy to know each other.

JM : What were the main problems you faced, actually doing the work?

HS : I had to be an invisible spy — an impossibility which I didn't particularly enjoy trying to achieve. What I found, actually doing the job, were a lot of practical difficulties, a lot of coping with my own reactions, of trying not to be embarrassed, at the same time as trying not to drop my camera or lose my films or take photographs with no film in the camera. I'm not a totally well-organised person, so I was quite preoccupied with that kind of thing, together with getting exposures right and so on. Having always been rather a perfectionist about things, I was simply out to do as good a job as I could. In a way, I deliberately avoided too much involvement in what Tom was after.

JM : You have said that, from quite early on, you were particularly interested in photographs of people who were not aware they were having their picture taken.

HS : Yes; though I don't think I started to take this sort of photograph myself until I was asked to do so. The first time I had to tackle the problems involved was in the work I did in Stepney. I was introduced by my probation officer friend to a family in Stepney, and I asked to photograph them. Well, the fact that they had to know that I was around made me very much aware of the comparison between the posed photograph and the unposed photograph; so I decided that I was going to try and make them so familiar with my presence that in the end I was photographing them — as far as possible — unposed and unaware that they were being photographed. I took a long time over this — many, many days — and I think in the end I succeeded in making them appear to be fairly natural, while disclosing their background, the circumstances in which they lived. I know I rather exploited the children. I would be pretending to photograph the children and suddenly swing round and take a picture of the adults when they weren't expecting it.

JM : But when you were there, you were clearly there as a photographer; you didn't participate in their lives in any way — you didn't, for example, eat a meal with them?

HS : Oh no, no, I was definitely someone from another planet. But I was accepted by them, and totally trusted in the sense that I was obviously doing a job that they respected — a job that they knew they might benefit from. But I've often wished since that I'd been able to devote more thought and more time to doing it better. I realise now how very much better I could have done it, although to a certain extent I'm surprised at how good the results were, now when I come to reprint them.

Looking back to the Stepney work, and then on to the Mass-Observation work, I always come back to the factor that I was constantly being faced with — the class distinction, the fact that I was somebody from another planet, intruding on another kind of life. And, of course, when something difficult or embarrassing occurred, one tended to revert to stereotype — as in that incident in the pub that I wrote up at the time, and which the Half Moon Gallery people got from the Mass-Observation Archive [reproduced in the notes to page 84]. My rather pompous response to the publican must have been pretty insufferable; and it's painful to read now. However much I tried, I could not hide characteristics of myself that I would have much preferred to keep hidden.

A constant feature of taking the kind of photograph we're talking about — even when people were unaware that they were actually being photographed — was a feeling that I was intruding, and that I was exploiting the people I was photographing, even when (as in Stepney) the aim explicitly was to help them.

JM : That being so, how would you account for the fact that, in looking at all the hundreds of photographs you took of people in Bolton and Blackpool and elsewhere, one never has a sense that you are using or exploiting your subjects?

HS : Well, just in normal living I do suddenly experience waves of identification and sympathy with certain people and situations that I see. For instance, today we were walking along Notting Hill Gate, and I saw that little boy on roller skates, skating very confidently but perhaps about to tumble over, though clearly soon to become a very competent and skilful skater: the empathy I feel at such moments is sometimes so strong that it almost makes me burst into tears. I think perhaps that was a strong motivation in my photography. Certainly, watching that roller-skating child, I would dearly have liked to take his photograph. And in doing so, of course, it would be very important that he didn't know it was being taken, because the whole atmosphere of his possible failure would then have vanished. The cause of the empathy would have been destroyed. Maybe it's wishful thinking in hindsight, but I reckon that, doing the job in Bolton, quite often I experienced that kind of sensation. It's a kind of identification that I experience most strongly if people are failing to do something; and, of course, that's a common enough sensation — if you see somebody like a beggar, somebody in very bad straits, somebody dying on the pavement, somebody who has had an accident. But I'm talking about something rather different, something experienced looking at ordinary people — it may be just a kind of face, or the way somebody wears a hat. Or if I see a person sitting eating in a café, who has dropped a lot of egg down their clothes, or got soup all over their moustaches, I don't feel I want to laugh. Perhaps that carried itself into photographing.

Actually, I very often hesitated much too much, because I didn't want to disclose predicaments, to embarrass people, I didn't want to introduce another element into what perhaps I was interpreting as their suffering. Furthermore, an important thing that I had learned through being attached to newspapers — through reacting against what newspapers were demanding — was that I had developed an attitude towards what I called caricature. That is, there was a very strong temptation to take a kind of photograph that was a caricature of its subject. You can catch people behaving in an out-of-the-ordinary, slightly comic way. It's like doing what Jacques Tati did in *Traffic* (which is a marvellous film, by the way), where he moves his camera down a traffic block and everybody's picking their noses. It's funny. People do pick their noses in traffic blocks. But it's not the entire truth; it's a caricature of the truth. So I was always alarmed at the possibility of doing that; I was at pains not to caricature people. It was a question, really, of recording normal behaviour.

Caricature is a trap that's always there to fall into. I remember later, when I was working for *Picture Post*, I went to a headmistresses' conference, and took a set of photographs of headmistresses looking like freaks, really. When I brought them back and showed them to Tom Hopkinson, he quite rightly said, 'These are caricature photographs. These are serious ladies: they may unintentionally look rather comic, but you've emphasised the comic aspect, and it really isn't fair to publish these.'

JM : Many of the photographs are of people who were poor, or extremely poor, and it seems certain that you were very conscious of their poverty; but there is no hint of you patronising your subjects.

HS : I think I can respond to what you're saying only by thinking of specific pictures. For instance, there is one [page 59] where there are two women, each wearing a hat, and they're photographed more or less full face (I don't know why they didn't see me), and they are looking at some goods for sale. They're clearly deciding — their facial expressions indicate that they are deciding — whether perhaps they can afford this thing, or whether they can't afford it. They can't make up their minds whether to buy, whether the thing's good stuff, whether the thing's trash. And I think I would have felt that those were exactly the sensations I would be going through if I was looking at, say, a watch in a window. I love watches. I'm always looking at watches, and I think I would be going through all those kinds of doubts and questions and confusions, asking myself whether I was going to be swindled.

Otherwise, my idea was always to capture an exact moment at which someone was going through some kind of action, or which was significant in some way — or more practically, I would simply have Tom Harrisson's voice ringing in my ears with a sentence like, 'People hold teacups in all kinds of ways — what do they do with their little fingers, are they sticking them out indicating they are socially superior, are they clutching the cup, are they . . .?' and so on. And that instruction would be enough to make me want to take the photograph. Very simple. Very practical.

JM : What equipment did you use in Bolton and Blackpool?

HS : Well, here again, it's very difficult to have an accurate recollection. To start with, I was using a very early Leica. You have to remember that those early cameras, although marvellous pieces of precision engineering for their time, were clumsy in comparison with modern automatic cameras. That is to say, there were very tedious operations. If you changed the lenses, you had to put in another viewfinder, which fixed into a slot in the camera, a viewfinder appropriate to the lens. There was no automatic focussing, there was no focussing visible through the viewfinder. You had to assess your distances, or you could slot a range-finder into the top of the camera, from which you took a reading and then adjusted your lens. So, in general, the equipment was pretty basic.

But that in a way had its advantages, because it meant that you had to get together a lot of experience which could tell you, literally in a moment, what your exposure should be according to the type of film you were using. The problem was that, in theory, the faster your film, the more grainy the negative would be, and this of course would show up in your print. A major trouble resulted, therefore, from the fact that you were trying to take shots in very bad light, relying only on the ordinary tungsten light available — in places like pubs and restaurants, election meetings, churches — taking all the kinds of interior shot that Tom Harrisson would imagine were going to illustrate the ordinary life of people. And you'd be up against the problem of long hand-held exposures. Technically, the whole operation needed much more skill than taking such photographs would today. Today, you've got much faster film, much finer grain, focussing in the viewfinder, exposure meters built into cameras — a whole range of technical advantages designed to eliminate the need for experience and thought, and the possibility of error.

JM : What did you use in addition to the Leica?

HS : The Leica I was using at the start of the Mass-Observation work was stolen, and I bought a Zeiss Contax 35. This means that most of the Mass-Observation work was taken with a very remarkable wide-angle lens called a Biogon, which fitted the Contax. The Biogon has a remarkable depth of focus, so that with an aperture of f6.3, it has a depth of focus of between five feet nine inches and infinity; and even with a fully open aperture, f2.8, it has a depth of focus of between six feet nine inches and twelve feet. My normal practice was to leave it set with as great a depth of focus as possible, which meant that I never had to think much about focussing. A lot of the interior photography for Mass-Observation depended on that particular lens. To sum up, my equipment consisted merely of one smallish 35mm camera and two lenses; and also I had made for me specially a leather case fitted with three compartments. This was very small, smaller than a miniature camera case, very beautifully made — it was possible to get such things done very cheaply in those days — with one compartment for an unexposed film, one for whichever lens I wasn't using, and the other for the viewfinder for the alternative lens.

The other lens was of normal focal length, a straightforward 50mm Tessar f2.8 for exterior shots. Quite apart from questions of light and focus, this was often not suitable for interior shots, because of its narrow angle of vision. If, for instance, you were shooting in a railway carriage or on top of a bus, you would not get the number of people in the photograph that you wanted.

JM : What about flash?

HS : I hated the whole idea of flash. I'll give you an actual situation: dog racing, taking place at night, with a crowd betting and watching and shouting. The moment you'd exposed one flash (and remember there wasn't, then, anything like electronic flash: you had a flash bulb, which made a considerable noise, and caused quite an alarming incident), you'd made everybody aware of your presence, of the fact that photography was going on. Without flash, you could probably operate in the same situation without ever being noticed. Also, generally I dislike very much the hard effects that flash produces, the very steep contrasts. I associate flash with the kind of photography that used to appear in society magazines like the *Tatler* and *Sphere*, where Commander Somebody-or-other is seen here with his latest girlfriend at such-and-such a night club —

grotesque photographs with very hard white faces and staring eyes.

JM : How much did you use filters?

HS : Well, the kind of photograph I was taking in Bolton was quite definitely not the 'beautiful photograph' type. My attachment to filters was entirely connected with skies and clouds, and buildings shining against dark skies. In Blackpool, it's true, I used filters quite a lot; in fact, there's not much interior photography from Blackpool.

JM : And the film you used?

HS : This was entirely a matter of using the fastest film you could get, so there was a continual search for the fastest film yet made. Quite a lot of photographers carried around two cameras, one with fast film, one with slow film. The slower the film, the sharper the image, the sharper the definition. But I didn't want to carry two cameras around, as that would have made what I was doing rather clumsy and obvious. So I was almost always using the fastest film I could, knowing that this would tend to produce quite a grainy image. Though, as a matter of fact, it's surprising how many of the photographs are not especially grainy, possibly because I used special fine-grain developers. The film I used most of the time was Agfa Isopan I.S.S., though occasionally I find Kodak Super X panchromatic film among the negatives.

JM : Did you keep a record of your subjects, shutter speeds and so on?

HS : I found one of the greatest problems was captioning. Captioning for a press photographer, for any photographer who is exposing quickly, who needs to work quickly, is absolute agony. It's often impossible to stop the whole sequence of action, even for a test exposure, and make a note in relation to a particular frame. In the end I just gave up completely, because this was something that made the whole operation clumsy. Then, later, I would try as best I could to caption collaboratively with Tom Harrisson, and with other people who might be able to recognise the location I'd been at. I haven't a clue where those records are now.

JM : To bring out more clearly the constraints you were operating under, can you say something about

the shutter speeds you would be using? What sort of speeds would the lighting in, say, a pub force on you?

HS : Film in those days was not nearly as sensitive to artificial light as it is now, so whenever you were relying on ordinary artificial light, you simply had to give the maximum hand-held exposure possible, all things considered. Take the occasion of people playing dominoes in a pub. You would sit there and observe that there were longish pauses, when the players were still looking at what was in their hands, and that there were sudden spurts of action. Gradually you would learn to anticipate the pauses. In all kinds of activities, people do arrive at moments when they are totally still, for a number of seconds or maybe less than a second, and from experience you learn to anticipate those moments. Even so, an exposure of a quarter of a second — which is a long time these days — was quite normal; and there were occasions when I had to be able to hold in my hand 'time' exposure of half a second or as much as a second. Of course, using a tripod was absolutely out, because it would have altered the whole character of the photography: you couldn't have avoided people posing.

JM : What was your attitude to movement visible in the final print?

HS : Nowadays, movement of a head, of a hand or foot, even movement of a whole figure is quite acceptable, and often is seen to add something to a photograph. In those days, maybe I wasn't being imaginative enough about it, but I tended to regard any movement in a photograph as a disqualification, and I would suppress the photograph. I now think that was often a wrong decision — as with one of the dominoes prints we're reproducing [page 81]. But inevitably, that whole idea about movement inhibited, or at least influenced, what you did. You were constantly on the search for a still moment, if only a split-second of equilibrium — as when a person is stepping on to a bus or tram.

A basic criterion of excellence in those days was sharpness of definition, absolute pin-sharpness. I remember the great battle which went on between 35mm operators and photographers using larger cameras. People were always trying to prove that fifteen by twelve enlargement from a 35mm negative would be just as sharp as a print produced by a large camera. There was a lot of wishful thinking around. I did in fact make some very big enlargements: I remember one of the Tyne Bridge, taken for the *Daily Mirror*, which was an attempt to prove that one could get very sharp definition. In the end, I think people have arrived at the conclusion that, if you want pin-sharp definition, you've got to use a big format camera.

JM : What about your procedures, aside from technical matters, when you were taking the Mass-Observation photographs?

HS : Well, it was all a matter of trickery, really, deceit. The great objective was usually to avoid suspicion, because people looking suspicious are people looking unnatural. For example, I remember a favourite trick, when I was using a range-finder to establish accurate focus, was to turn at right angles to the subject of the photograph and do my focussing on an object a similar distance away: having done that, I would swing round and take my shot very quickly. Another technique was to do a continuous pan, starting from a point exactly opposite the subject, shooting at the moment you arrived at the subject and then continuing the swing right round: nobody knew quite what you were up to — you were simply experimenting with your camera. Then there was the obvious technique of concealing the camera, hung from your neck by a piece of string, and allowing the lens to emerge from a very shabby raincoat, or similar garment. In order to work the camera I had a hole in my right-hand pocket — or there may have been a hole in both pockets, I can't remember. It was a very obvious disguise. One plan, which I never operated, was to have a briefcase with a hole cut in it, with some means of judging the correct aim of the lens — helped, of course, by the marvellous wide-angle lens — and then simply to fiddle around with the briefcase in some innocent way and take the photograph. I rather think Cartier-Bresson did something like that.

JM : Did you take photographs without actually looking through the viewfinder?

HS : Yes, quite a lot were taken by just aiming the camera from, say, waist-height, or with the camera resting on a table at which I was sitting. That would be after having done test shots, to discover correct angles for any particular lens. There again there was a great advantage in the wide-angle lens. My intention at the time was merely to produce a negative from which I could select a small portion to print as the final photograph — in other words, to treat cropping as entirely legitimate. It so happens that nowadays fashion dictates that cropping is almost not allowed. Everybody is very much at pains to show that they composed the photograph in full frame. In conforming to this fashion when reprinting the Mass-Observation photographs, it's rather curious how often the full frame proves more interesting, more effective, than the original cropped version.

JM : How do you account for the fact that your aim was so accurate?

HS : Just experience, I think. Just by a process of testing, developing, printing, and re-testing. And incidentally, resting the camera on a table — in a restaurant or pub, for example — gave the possibility of longer exposure, hand-held: the table acted as a kind of tripod.

JM : Sometimes, then, your technique would be to make people aware that you had a camera, that you *were* a photographer, but to allay their anxieties in some way?

HS : If you were a stranger in a place where people knew each other, such as a pub, you were immediately a focus of interest. They would eye you closely and see you had a camera, and then you would try various forms of deception — like just fiddling with the camera, twisting the settings, taking the lens out, putting it back, committing awful crimes like blowing into it (or rather, pretending to blow into it), cleaning the viewfinder. People merely looked at you, thought, 'Oh, there's a bloke with a camera, he's cleaning it up,' and then got on with whatever they were doing, and you became part of the landscape. Those were ruses so to speak.

Other occasions came under the category of the patient method, where you settled down for anything up to an hour or an hour and a half, and

became part of the scenery. When people were no longer taking any notice, then you produced your camera and started operating. This was particularly necessary in streets, for instance. You could just be leaning against a lamppost, or waiting for a bus. And there is a whole series of pictures of people window-shopping: I can remember hanging around in shop entrances, and sometimes, when the shop was on a corner, shooting through two layers of glass on to a person round the corner. There is also a sequence of photographs of people getting on to trams. There you've got a lucky set-up, because people are anxious about their time, about being punctual, they are preoccupied with themselves, with getting on to the tram, and are not looking round at what's going on. Certain situations play into your hands in that way.

JM : Did you use long focus lenses at all?

HS : In those days, a long focus — otherwise known as a telephoto — lens was an enormous contraption, sometimes as much as two feet long, very thick and heavy. It required a tripod, and couldn't be made invisible in any circumstances. Recent technology has devised very small telephoto attachments, whereby, if you have a camera that will take interchangeable lenses, you can insert an intermediate lens, on top of which goes your ordinary lens, and you've got a mini-telephoto lens. But once you start playing around with things like that, the amount of equipment you're carrying makes for a lot of trouble. I've found, on the whole, that I have rejected all that equipment. In Regent Street yesterday, I saw a man with a tripod over his shoulder, a camera attached to the tripod, a large case slung over his shoulder *and* a hand-held case. Well, he's probably got four or five interchangeable lenses, electronic flash equipment of all kinds, and his presence is announced very clearly wherever he goes. Or there's somebody like Leni Riefensthal — who was a Nazi but a marvellous photographer — in recent years she has used as many as seven cameras at once, some of them worked by motor, and requiring two or three assistants. Of course, this is the thing nowadays: a motorised camera, which is something like a cine-camera, taking whole sequences of exposures from which you choose your final frame. Which reminds me of my time at the *Mirror*, when I used to see my colleagues shooting away like mad — for example, at a society wedding, where there might be up to fifteen photographers present, with all of those fifteen photographers *all* taking the same subject, pretty well the same photograph, *all* of them shooting one frame after another. I think that's just daft. So I made a kind of ascetic rule for myself, that I wouldn't get involved in taking huge sequences of shots, and would try to confine myself to one shot, or two or three at the most.

JM : Among the photographs from Bolton and Blackpool, are there any which you can quite specifically remember taking?

HS : Well, remembering is altogether very difficult. I find my memory of much that went on has not just faded but disappeared. For example, I can remember nothing of that incident in the pub that I wrote up. I can't recall the incident; I can't recall writing the report. When you first read it out to me, I thought it was somebody else's description. But I do remember another incident in a pub — the one where the man is holding up his hand [page 84]. And I can recall taking the funeral photographs [pages 119-24], because I suffered very much from a feeling that I was exploiting grief. Also, I do remember Tom Harrisson went potty about a religious sect, which has a baptismal celebration involving total immersion in a tank built into the floor: he was mad keen to get photographs of total immersion, he thought it was hilarious. Actually, I was slung out after taking one rather poor shot. But no, generally it's difficult to remember, it's such a long time ago. I can persuade myself that I can recall taking certain shots; but I can't really.

JM : What about that photograph of the workers coming out of the mill [page 50]? There's either nobody, or just possibly one person, looking at the camera.

HS : I think I can guess, if not remember, the circumstances surrounding that shot. You knew that this happened regularly, every day, at precisely the same time: sirens blew, bells rang and the gates were opened by the keeper. You knew this was going to happen. I've said in the past that I did the

shot with a pan. But I think I probably did it with a concealed camera, simply standing on the other side of the road. I would have done all the preliminary work of focus, angle of vision and so on, and I was simply there, ready to take the shot before anyone noticed. That was a relatively easy situation, really.

JM : What about domestic interiors? There's only one that I know of in the entire Mass-Observation collection [page 54].

HS : Yes, a lot of people have asked that question. It was something that we did very much discuss. The moment you start thinking about domestic interiors, you're involved in quite a lot of planning and organisation, finding a willing family: and clearly you can't go into someone's house and remain unnoticed, so immediately you're up against the possibilities of play-acting, a kind of falsity. And you're under suspicion. 'Why do they want to come and photograph *me*?' You might find that a husband and wife, faced with the possibility, might have a conversation beginning on the lines, 'Can't let him see that dirty old carpet, must wash the curtains, the dog's absolutely filthy, get *him* washed, must iron Mary's dress,' and so on. You are then going into a false situation. We talked about this, and decided against it. I'd had the Stepney experience, and been reasonably successful there, but Tom was preoccupied with the likelihood of influencing, disturbing, the details of people's habitual behaviour, and literally giving a false picture.

There is that one photograph, of the bathing of the baby. But that was arranged by special request from someone in Bolton who came and worked for Mass-Observation. Of course, the picture looks prearranged, posed, although it does have quite a quality about it. The fact that there's a baby being bathed in a zinc tub by an open fire — those circumstances were not arranged. But everybody present knew this was happening, except perhaps the baby! A lot of people have said it's a lack, that there are no other domestic interiors. But I can see so many lacks. I've said this before: there should have been five photographers working, not one. I myself made only about half a dozen visits, of not more than a week each time.

JM : Why didn't you go into factories very much, even though you had the possibility of easy access, through Tom Harrisson's industrial benefactors?

HS : Again, it's very difficult to be unnoticed in a factory. You have to get permission, clearly; and from the word go, you've got a foreman or deputy manager or some functionary asking himself, 'Is there anything we don't want publicised? Are we breaking any regulations? Photographs might be used in evidence against us.' So immediately people are very wary and on their best behaviour. The occasional factory visits we made were very much prearranged. I think in all the factory shots you can read into the photograph the fact that I had asked someone to be doing a certain thing, or standing in a certain position, to disclose some aspect of the work. I'm thinking in particular of a rather good photograph of a girl handling the things on which the yarns are wound [page 47]. I can almost hear my own voice saying, 'Stand like this, don't look at the camera, let the camera see the thing you're holding.' I was more interested in the secret photograph. But also it bored me to be trailed around. You were always *taken around*. And whenever you entered a factory space, provided it wasn't so noisy that your arrival went unnoticed, everybody always looked up and put on their best expressions — 'Which is the best side of my face?' kind of reaction. I had done a lot of that kind of work, for one reason or another, working for the *Mirror*.

JM : On the other hand — and this is a general point — much of what the Mass-Observation observers were writing down in their notebooks could have been more easily recorded by the camera, *whether or not* people were aware that they were being photographed.

HS : This is true. It's quite true that Tom would literally search the whole surface of a collection of photographs for information, about small details — the number of rings that people were wearing on their fingers, whether they were wearing horn-rimmed glasses, how many people had beards, how many didn't have beards, how many people had cloth caps in a football crowd. It was factual data, of every kind, that he wanted from photographs.

JM : Given this, and given his express concern to

record reality in as 'objective' a way as possible, why did Tom Harrisson encourage painters to come to Bolton? Why, indeed, did he encourage you to draw and paint as well as to take photographs?

HS : I've never fully understood why he had painters. Certainly, he put photography and painting into two quite separate compartments — though, at the same time, he was very responsive to a well composed photograph: he was very encouraging to me in that respect. Without doubt, his impulse was to encourage a variety of approaches. For instance, just before the war he was planning an expedition to Borneo, for which I took a course in Anthropology at the London School of Economics, preparing to go on this, as a photographer again. On that expedition, he was going to have not only painters but sculptors and dancers, ballet dancers and poets. He was going to have a whole group of creative people. Well now, if only Tom were alive to explain his reasons.

Actually, even with the photographs, I think he never quite knew what he was going to get out of them. From the beginning, he was obsessed with collecting as many data, as much raw material of all kinds, as possible, and he saw the photographs as part of that: in a sense, the main thing was that they were there. But I think his motives were decidedly mixed. For example, his interest in grotesqueries — as with total immersion — was not just a matter of recording things. The caricature element appealed to him; and it didn't worry him particularly that a set of photographs might not properly — fully — represent somebody's religion. I resisted this tendency as much as I could. I tried to concentrate on simply recording information. Over the years, Tom came to see the photographs from time to time, and he was always very enthusiastic. He had a standard thing to say: 'One day these will be fantastic, they will be of great use. At the moment we haven't enough money to produce a book, but it's very important to keep them.'

Photography and its Limits

In June 1981, Humphrey Spender went back to Bolton and Blackpool with a Granada Television crew, to re-create, for a film about his Mass-Observation photographs, the ways in which he had taken the original pictures.

JM : What did the experience of doing the Granada film make you feel about having given up professional photography?

HS : My feeling about being made to take photographs again really confirmed what I have felt over the years. All the time I'm going around, just in normal living, I'm continually seeing the possibility of marvellous photographs, and always that response is followed immediately by a second one: 'Thank goodness I haven't got to take them!'

There are a number of reasons for not wanting to take photographs. First, there's the practical one that, if you take a photograph, you've got to develop it, and then you've got to print it, and that can be very tedious. But more importantly, there are other things I'm glad to escape, like the familiar feeling of being thought to be a spy. Because the kind of photograph that interests me most is a revelation of human behaviour, one is always liable to be found out, kicked out — or worse. In Morocco, I had a bucket of water thrown over me; and on another occasion, a knife was thrown at me. Even though the reasons in Morocco were something to do with the 'evil eye', I don't think they were all that different from the reasons operating in this country. People just don't like being recorded when they are not showing, so to speak, the best side of their faces.

But apart from the hostility — and perhaps occasionally, physical violence — that you're courting, with all the attendant embarrassments, there's the sense of intruding on people's privacy, and sometimes their suffering — of exploiting them. And this connects with another reason why I gave up professional photography. When you're photographing people, unless they're friends or relations, you set up a temporary relationship which I found myself disliking more and more — the artificiality of it. And worst of all, when you're photographing people

without them knowing — which is the form of photography that still interests me most — you eliminate *all* relationship. One of the reasons why photographers often confine themselves to *things* is that you don't lay yourself open to the same emotional hazards when you're photographing things. With the exception of the Sunday excursion — taking pictures of relations and friends — I've confined myself to things for many years; and that has been mainly to provide sources, to feed my painting and designing in all sorts of ways.

At the same time, I want to stress that the photographers I continue to appreciate and admire most are those concerned with humanity — those who, in disclosing humanity and human behaviour, also disclose part of their own attitude towards humanity and human behaviour. And I am not referring only to those who happen to adopt my style of photography, that of the 'unobserved observer'. There are photographers who take their subjects, tell them they are going to be photographed, sit them in front of the camera, and who — with no kind of prettification or titivation, by absolutely straightforward means — project statements about human behaviour and human appearance, and about themselves, which are extremely interesting.

What I admire most of all is something very rarely arrived at: the sort of concern I've been talking about, expressed in a fusion of a profound knowledge of the capabilities of photography, the techniques of photography, with the taking of a great deal of trouble — as Cartier-Bresson did, as André Kertesz did.

Coming back to the Granada trip, I was interested to discover that, alongside the old feelings of apprehension and embarrassment, a lot of the old skills came back, too. For instance, I realised that, even shooting from the chest, without lifting the camera to my eye, I was assessing and waiting for a future arrangement of bodies, so to speak. There would be a gap towards which somebody was approaching from a distance, and I would know instinctively how long it would be before that person filled that gap; and I found myself waiting for that to happen. (Provided it wasn't too long a wait, of course; in which case one would have become an object of suspicion.) I realised that there was a lot of composing, a lot of refusing to take the shot unless I knew that what I wanted was going to happen. Reflecting on this, and on what I'd come to see in reprinting the Worktown negatives, I had a stronger sense of the results of having painted from the age of six, and of having been trained as an architect.

Composition, frames of reference, verticality, horizontality, balance and rhythm — all these things sound rather boring when tutors start talking about them, and one is inclined to say, 'Oh shut up, for God's sake!' But you do eventually train yourself into an awareness of this mysterious thing called composition. And in Bolton and Blackpool again, I found myself waiting for the picture to compose itself. Waiting, too, for the moment when a human being comes to a point of rest, remains still and it's the moment to press the button. Another thing was that, in the days when there were no exposure meters, when cameras were much less sophisticated and you didn't carry around a great amount of equipment, you really had to train yourself into recognising light conditions and knowing about depth of focus (there are very few amateur photographers who have bothered to use the depth of focus scale built into the camera). I did become very well grounded in this, so that I can set the camera almost without thinking; and this enables you to concentrate on other matters. I think all these things can be described in terms of accumulated experience.

JM : Can you say more about Cartier-Bresson? It's useful to talk about him because he is somebody who is — relative to many other distinguished photographers — very well known, he is generally very highly regarded, and he is also very highly regarded by you. What is it about his work which is its distinction, which makes it unique or rare, for you?

HS : He was one of the first people to use miniature cameras for 'candid camera' photography. For that alone he shines. But what I like about Cartier-Bresson is precisely the acceptance of what is there, what is all around one to be discovered — to be discovered with patience and observation. He also seems to disclose an absolutely perfect sense of timing, when to actually take the photograph, when to click the shutter. I'd love to know — something

that is very revealing about any photographer – – whether he made a great many exposures of any given subject. My guess is that he usually didn't.

As for his uniqueness or otherwise, I really don't know. I think his excellence is confirmed by the fact that he started a whole school of photographers, who have appreciated him and consciously followed in his footsteps. But if you were to put me to the test of pointing out the Cartier-Bresson amongst a lot of others by some of the marvellous young photographers that are around today, I think I'd probably fail to find it. In saying that, I'm really making a comment about photography generally. I'm reminded of my experience of that huge exhibition of Cartier-Bresson fairly recently at the Hayward Gallery. There were several hundred photographs in it, and I went in a state of great excitement because of my enormous admiration for Cartier-Bresson. Yet after about twenty-five photographs, I found myself quite incapable of looking at any more. So I resorted to the exercise of forcing myself to go round the whole exhibition, trying to decide which were the best twenty. Which eventually I managed to do. But I think they made a great mistake in showing quite so many prints. Photography just doesn't stand up to that kind of huge exposure.

There is an attempt nowadays by art critics to raise photography to the level of painting, which I cannot go along with. I think the attempt is partly inspired by the art market, about which one is permanently suspicious. The higher the status generally accorded to photography, the more valuable photographs become as commodities. You hear one gallery-owner saying to another, 'Are you into photography yet?', as though all art galleries will have their photographic section one day. The financial boys reckon they've found an inexhaustible source of collector's pieces. But I stand back from the equation of photography with painting, and look at it with great astonishment. For example, the prices put on some of my own vintage prints [i.e. prints made immediately after the photographs were taken, forty or more years ago] seem to me absolutely daft.

I'm not saying that all critics are activated by the market-place. But only this week, listening to a cri-

tics' programme on the radio while I was bungling away in the darkroom, probably pouring one wrong solution into another, I suddenly heard a voice say, 'Humphrey Spender has made a formidable contribution to documentary photography.' Well, I thought, 'Marvellous!' — it's lovely having people say things like that. But I do find it quite difficult to take seriously — to take seriously the extent to which other people take it seriously. If one chooses one of the best photographers ever — let us *say* Cartier-Bresson — could one mention him in the same breath as Goya, or Picasso? I really don't think so. Yet there are many people who do — many people, even, who swoon at the thought of Cecil Beaton.

JM : Why do you think you value photography less highly than many other people do?

HS : I think a lot about why I tend to react in a rather hostile way to photography. I'm not alone, of course. David Hockney, for instance, has described exhibitions of photographs as boring in comparison with exhibitions of paintings: boring in the extent to which there's a uniformity of surface texture, a uniformity in the gradation of tone. He said that a national gallery filled with the best photographs of all time would have a certain monotony about it. On the other hand, if you go to the extremes reached by a lot of art student photographer-types, who are thronging the photography departments of art schools, and say — particularly now colour processing has become so sophisticated — that you can regard photography as a creative process in exactly the same way as you regard the use of brushes and tubes of paint and canvases, then I feel bound to reply that you are taking a process and making a final result which is an *imitation* of something produced by one of the orthographic processes: etching, aquatint, mezzotint, lithography, engraving, ordinary painting, and the rest; or even an imitation of some other artist's work. Why do you have to have a camera intervening in this? It's at that point that I begin to say that this is a misuse of the camera.

My feeling about the proper functions of the camera is that it should be concerned primarily with recording and providing information. It is often better at doing that than any other medium — though it's important to stress that it's impossible to exclude the person in charge of the camera from most kinds of picture: indeed, that can have its own great interest. (Photography can also produce great distortions, especially if you take into account the making of the print and the possibilities of cropping, in addition to the actual taking of the picture.) The Worktown photographs were taken to provide information. The fact that they have become — particularly the original prints — 'art objects' in frames makes me uneasy. And that's a kind of feeling that increasingly is disturbing some photographers.

There's a fundamental sense in which photography is too *easy*. It so happens that at the moment, in one small town in Essex, I have an exhibition of paintings and a separate exhibition of photographs. People have made many, many more comments about the photographs than about the paintings; and they tend to be more appreciative of the photographs. Now you may say that's because I've produced a lot of dud paintings. But I think it has a lot to do with the fact that photographs are generally more accessible. Which in turn leads me to the fact that, in some way or other, in some degree or other, a photograph is always convincing. In taking photographs, you simply cannot make a total, hopeless mess of it. Whatever you do — provided you put a film in your camera, provided you remember to press the button and so on — something comes out which is in a certain way convincing. There is an image of reality. It may be tilted sideways, or it may be pointing upwards, or you may have missed what you were aiming at, but there *is* an image of reality. You'll get somebody standing in front of a drawing and saying, 'That's a bloody bad drawing. He's bungled this, and he hasn't got that right: really, he should never have put that thing up, it's totally incompetent.' You never get anbody making that kind of criticism of a photograph. The automatic convincingness of photography is one side of the coin. The other side is that painting, for instance, offers you a far greater range of creative thinking: a photograph can never arrive at the same level of creative intelligence as a great painting.

As a profession, photography has for me too many easy answers. If I try and answer the question

— which I've tried many times — 'Why did you give up photography?', in addition to the reasons I've already indicated, I have to say it's partly a matter of challenges. Consider just the printing part of the process — which, to my mind, is the most creative part. Any given negative, printed by someone who didn't understand it, who didn't understand why one took it and who is printing it as an ordinary routine job (this has quite often happened to my negatives), can lose all its interest. But at the same time you *know* perfection can be achieved; and this knowledge is very different from what it would be better to call a *lack of knowledge* in painting, because when you're painting you know that you'll never achieve what lies in the back of your mind, that you can never achieve perfection. The gap between mind and hand, which is unbridgeable in painting, is bridgeable in photography, provided you can flog your mind enough. The unattainable challenge is to me much more stimulating. You have got to go on just because you're striving for something you know you'll never achieve. Striving for the perfect print becomes ultimately boring and tedious. It can also be physically exhausting.

Producing the print that you know is attainable can take ages. Just one version can take an hour or more. What's called 'dodging' — masking parts of the negative with your hand under the enlarger, to hold back one bit of the negative, or bring up another — is a tiring business, quite often requiring concentration and muscular control for minutes on end. Sometimes you have to make cut-out masks, which is very time-consuming to do properly. And then, out of the darkness, there drops — unnoticed, of course — something from the ceiling or a passing insect; and only when you've developed the print do you discover it's unusable. This is quite apart from putting the paper in the wrong way round, or not straight.

In painting, not only is every mark immediately visible, and immediately giving rise to developing trains of thought; but you can drop everything if you wish, wander round the garden, think, and no harm is done: you can come back to it, perhaps freshened and all the better for having paused. In a darkroom, you can't stop; you can't read, you can't relax the

muscular tension, you've got to go on. You can have the radio on, but even that may distract you from the necessary concentration.

It's different if you're highly successful in financial terms. Photographers like Cecil Beaton have solved the problem of the tedium of the darkroom by being able to afford assistants. It is perfectly possible to train a darkroom assistant to reproduce exactly your own ideas, your own techniques for perfect printing. In my opinion, it's never possible for a painter. I think this is shown if you look back to what are called schools of painting — to big paintings which are known to have been carried out by assistants of such artists as Raphael and Rubens. Nowadays, people generally find more vitality in the sketch produced by Rubens than in the enormous finished picture largely painted by his assistants.

There is, of course, a certain excitement — sometimes a great excitement — when you've taken a film out of the developing tank, seen a very remarkable negative, and know that you're going to be able to get a good print. But the excitement can go dead as you realise the effort that will have to be put into getting the final result, and the tedium of that effort.

I should perhaps add that I get most satisfaction from printing the sort of photographs I took for Mass-Observation, just because their purpose is to disclose information. That determines how you manipulate the print, and you know clearly what you're after. Compare that with a photograph I've taken recently, of a frozen puddle in which you can see all kinds of associative figures. In this frozen puddle, I can see a little man in a woolly cap, and a diver coming up from the depths with tubes and other things attached to him. Faced with that negative, I know that, with skilful printing, I could emphasise or suppress any particular part of it in my final print. I have in fact printed it, and got an interesting picture; but I realise there are endless things I could have done with it. I could spend the rest of my life printing that one negative, and getting a hundred and sixty-five thousand different versions of it. Now with the Mass-Observation negatives you are limited in the extent to which you can manipulate the whole thing. You've got to show the reasons for which the photograph was taken. You've got to show people's faces, people's behaviour; you've got to show their clothing and other details.

With photography, given its strengths and limitations, I prefer to be pinned down. I experience a sense of real fear and panic when I think simply of the number of photographs waiting to be taken, the limitless amount of film there is to be bought, the variety of lenses, the endless ways you can deal with subjects — but always in a medium that is *always* convincing, whatever you produce.

Alongside that sensation, I experience another one, to do with the number of photographs that are actually being taken — the fact that nowadays thousands of people are taking photographs every second of the day. There is something enervating about that. Partly because it means that the whole activity has become more and more competitive. Partly because of the feeling that one is simply playing into the hands of the big industrial empires — exemplified by the story of the junk in Hong Kong

harbour. I was photographing it when somebody nudged me and said, 'Do you realise that junk was put there by Kodak?' After that, I couldn't help suggesting that the Royal Wedding had been organised by Ilford. Just think of all the photographic activity that must have gone on around it. It's really a marvel.

JM : Finally, could we come back to the *uses* of photography, in connection with causes that you support — or are hostile to?

HS : Articles that I have read in photographic journals and elsewhere have helped to convince me that photography can be a very serious weapon — can, if wrongly used in a propagandist way, have the power of a bomb. I'm now even more aware than I used to be of the dangers in using photography in the way Goebels did during the second world war, as a State propaganda weapon. But on the other hand, in so far as I still want to do photography in a public way, I want to use it to affect life, to improve

life. For example, I'm finding that pictures I've taken recently of the active destruction of the countryside have inspired me to carry on and do more, to go on using the camera. (As you will have gathered, part of my attitude to photography derives from simple physical laziness.) It's quite likely that I shall do some photography for the nuclear disarmament movement. If asked, I would certainly stir myself up to help in that way.

JM : So would you say that your position is now very similar to what it was forty or forty-five years ago: one of willingness to do what is asked of you?

HS : Yes, for causes similar to Stepney, Mass-Observation, working for *Left Review*, photographing the Hunger Marchers, photographing the Mosley meeting at the Albert Hall. Subject, of course, to the onset of age, physical disability — or general senility.

Street Life

30 May procession : two photographs

Work

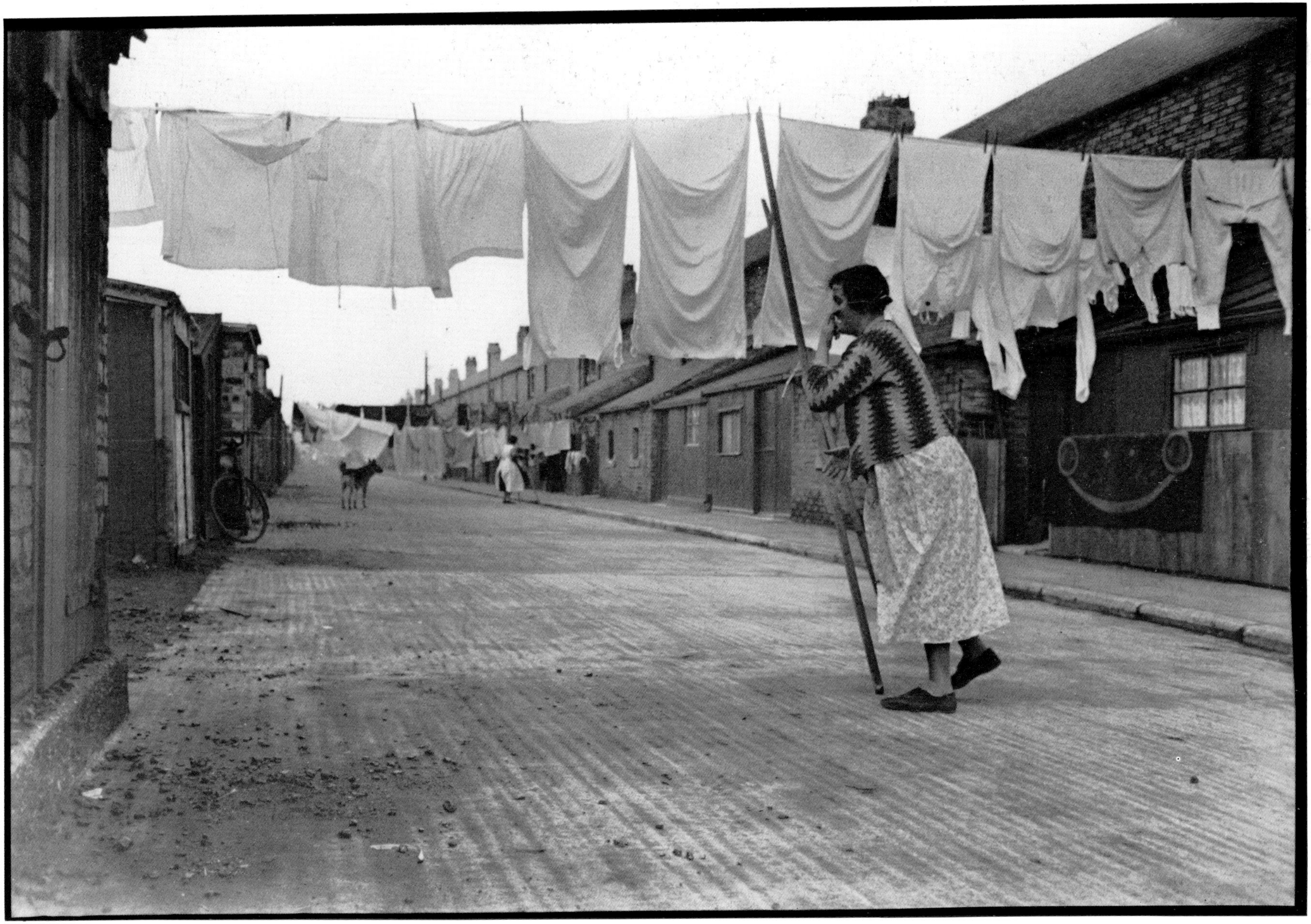

PROF. H. TAYLER M.N.C.S.
WORKING MANS
HAIR SPECIALIST
PREVENTS
ALOPECIA · RINGWORM · SCRUFF · DANDRUFF
Laboratories   72 GORDON St
Manchester

62   Apprentices' strike : two photographs

Sport

68

70 Greyhound track : two photographs

72 Sports day : two photographs

74

Parks

Drinking

Elections

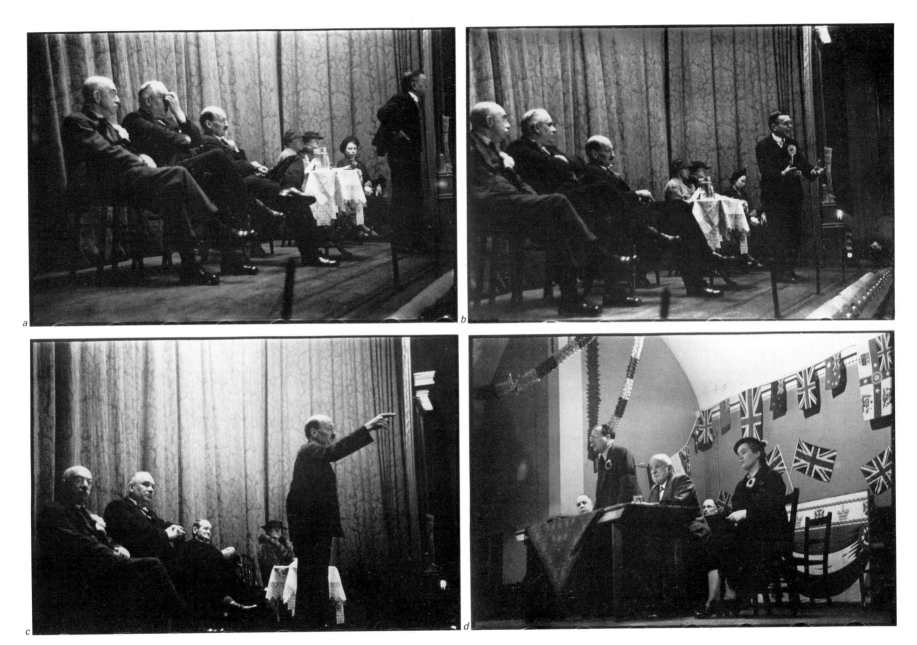

a–c Labour Party meeting; *d* National Government meeting **89**

THE
PLUMS
RADIO TIMES
SCOTLAND YARD
WAR ON
VICE
WEEKLY
BOLTON
CHELSEA
Empire
News

Blackpool

116

119

Funeral

Notes

Abbreviations used: HG — Harry Gordon, HS — Humphrey Spender; BR — Britain Revisited, PP — The Pub and the People; M-O — observer's report or draft chapter in the Mass-Observation Archive. For further details, see the Introduction.

Page 25. This view of Lum Street gasometer was taken from the top of Bolton parish church, St. Peter's, in the town centre. 'In Bolton, I was certainly not out to take the "beautiful photograph", but occasionally it happened — I couldn't resist it.' (HS)

Street Life

28/1. Not only the trams but also the rails, wires and ornate supporting posts associated with them (see p.44) have disappeared.

28/2. 'I would assume these were ordinary working-class women, probably retired from working now, and just doing their shopping. My assumption is that this is on a Tuesday or a Thursday, Market Day, and that's why they've congregated there. They're dressed up because it's Market Day.' (HG) This photograph was taken from the car whose wing mirror can be seen in the foreground.

30 & 31. 'I would say this is the May procession, going round the bounds of the parish.' (HG)

33. 'This great big flagged area is where we used to go dancing and playing on . . . The road blocks are "blue sets", blue granite — very slippery, them, very greasy when it were wet, especially when you had clogs on, with irons nailed to the bottom.' (HG) 'I definitely decided to wait until "3 smart girls" came by, in whatever form; and I was delighted with what came about. But they might have been three mill girls — or three old ladies.' (HS)

36 & 37. Different views of the same corner.

39. 'He's saying, "I'm making a picture, and if there's anything left I'll make one for you." ' (HG)

40. 'This is a back street near Burnden Park football ground, where Bolton Wanderers play. The owners are watching the match whilst the machines are being looked after for a nominal fee.' (HG)

41. 'The mill in the distance, at the end of the street, is one of Barlow and Jones's mills. I lived in the second house facing that mill.' (HG) 'That's the same Barlow — Sir William Barlow — as Tom Harrisson got a lot of money from for Mass-Observation. And his daughter, Penelope Barlow, came and worked for Tom.' (HS)

42. 'It's top and whip, that. The season must have been in. Nobody ever found out how top and whip seasons came. They just came and went.' (HG) The markings on the pavement are for hopscotch. 'I play these games when I see other people playing them or when I see the things in the shop windows and it is then that we play these games for we copy what they have been doing.' (Boy aged 8 — M-O)

45. One of only two flash photographs in the book — taken after the same closing-time as the one on p.85. On p.18, Humphrey Spender explains why he seldom used flash.

Work

'The great majority of workers, both sexes, in Worktown have jobs which involve standing or walking about, mainly in artificially hot or damp atmospheres, tropical all the year round, so noisy that a lip-reading system has developed as language.' (PP, p.105) 'The saying "A woman's place is in the home" is still current in Worktown where 44 per cent of the adult women earn their own or their families' livings directly (over half these work in cotton mills).' (PP, p.106)

46. These women are operating reeling machines, which produce hanks such as those behind the woman in the foreground. This and the following three photographs were taken in the group of Barlow and Jones mills of which one can be seen at the end of the street on p.41.

47. This woman is about to replace one of the bobbins on the spinning frame. It is an 'intermediate' frame, now superseded, in the spinning process of twisting the thread while making it at once thinner, longer and stronger.

48. These women are hemming towels, in one of the lower buildings. The buildings that house earlier parts of the process had a number of storeys so that one engine could easily drive machines on a number of floors at once.

49. The huge reels are referred to as 'warps', since they carry the warp — i.e. the threads extended lengthwise in the loom and usually twisted harder than the threads (the weft or woof) that are interwoven with them to form the cloth.

52. This and the next photograph were taken from opposite ends of the street, which is the one on the right on p.41. 'Every Monday, there were a row in this street, because the coalmen couldn't deliver coal, and they hated it.' (HG)

53. 'It's quite possible, by the way, that she's done this washing, but it's somebody else's — either to get half-a-crown [12½p] for a basket of washing, or she's borrowed the clothes and washed them free, because she'll put them in the pawn and use the money until next Friday. This is what used to happen. This is the way we lived. It wasn't so bad in the thirties as it was when I were younger; but it was happening.' (HG)

54. The only domestic interior in the whole collection of Mass-Observation photographs (see p.20 for the reasons). 'This is a tiled fireplace, which weren't in a lot of houses at that time, or when I were younger. Now Davenport Street, they used to be people as could afford that. The next street to Davenport Street was actually Clarence Street. My mother used to go cleaning in Clarence Street, and I used to go and assist her. (I had to do. We never got away scot-free, you know.) The people who lived in Davenport Street then, they weren't middle-class, but they were on that side. Him I used to visit in the third house along there, he was an optician by trade, and I used to go for political meetings, preparing for a meeting in the Town Hall square, on the steps. That'd be in the early thirties. But when Mass-Observation were there, it were going down then, going down rapidly. And instead of one family living in a house, you might have two or three families, working-class people. Davenport Street started going down by virtue of the inhabitants as were coming into it. You see what happened was, first they started building council houses farther out; and then people with money realised which way wind was blowing, so they were having houses built on the outskirts, too. But Clarence Street kept itself for a long time. When they were demolishing one house in Clarence Street, and they come to go through the house to see whether there were anything worthwhile saving, what they found was a full-size billiard table, with snooker balls on, the lot. Now I'm telling you this to show you what type of people lived there one time. . . There was one thing I didn't like about Davenport Street where they [Mass-Observation] used to go — I used to keep away from it if I could. It always smelt of something, which I don't like, and I've never liked in my life: fish and chips. They lived off fish and chips.' (HG) '85 Davenport Street, one in a continuous row of bug-ridden houses . . .' (BR, p.29)

55. The paving-stones next to the step are being scrubbed and wiped clean, and the step itself is whitened with a donkey stone — an artificial stone for cleaning and whitening flagstones, steps etc. ('the rag-and-bone men, quite often they'd give you a donkey stone or two for what they took away' [HG]). 'If they got a little bit posh, they'd go right down to the kerbstone.' (HG) 'There is no light in the subject, it's completely flat; the negative is quite without contrast. It was taken either early in the morning or late in the day. So I had to use super-contrast paper, which is necessarily grainy and shows up all defects that much more readily.' (HS)

56. 'I can see my wife stood here now saying, "I wonder whether those shoes'll fit my husband." And she'd say, "No, I've no money — bugger him!" . . . My wife used to like going to these places. She loved this sort of business. In fact, she went so often, a woman said to her one Tuesday, she said, "I'm not so well. Will you look after my stall for me a minute?" And she went across to a pub for a couple of whiskies, and my wife were on stall when I went alooking for her, looking after the stall for this woman . . . They're good, these photos. I'll tell you something. I'd love my wife to be able to come and see these — somebody bring her back from heaven. She'd love these.' (HG)

58. 'You get people coming and selling stuff on the open market, persuading people to buy — you know, you start off at a pound and finish up at fourpence. One bloke was supposed to be selling shaving material and, because he'd got no customers, he said to people, "What do you want, hot water with it?" So he sold a pile of it after — shaving soap, cheap razor blades and all that caper. . . This bloke here's selling some sort of medicine. [A companion picture shows an array of bottles.] He's mixed a concoction. Now whether they're going to cure pregnancy or something like that, these women, I don't know. I would assume that their boat's gone down, wouldn't you? From the looks of them, you know. But this fellow, definitely, is like the fellow that's curing alopecia [p.61]. He's curing boils, children or what have you — flat feet, and stopping you from being pregnant.' (HG)

62. 'There's only one thing you go on strike about, and that's money. . . In engineering, you can't bring apprentices out on strike: they have to do it themselves. In years gone by, there were only ever two apprentices' strikes; and this one, in 1937, apprentices on Clydeside walked out of their workshops, and the strike spread all over the country, and came to Bolton via Manchester. Two apprentices came to the factory gates at William Wadsworth's. The apprentices walked out and brought out the apprentices at Hick Hargreaves', Bolton. Then on to Queen's Park to have the meeting pictured here.' (HG)

63. 'It was a popular place with the unemployed in those days — every paper free, and every morning paper was there. They always used to have them up on the stands, so you wouldn't sit down. They clipped these papers in.' (HG)

Sport

64. The bowling green on this and the following page belonged to a public house, the Gibraltar Rock. 'Usually pub bowling greens were looked after a lot better than the others, because it drew custom.' (HG) 'The game played locally is "crown bowls", which takes place on greens of fine turf that are not quite level, having a "crown", or slight convexity, that raises the centre of the green a few inches higher than the edges. (In the south bowls are almost invariably played on a flat green.) The game is played by teams or individuals bowling round wooden balls (about 8 inches in diameter) at another smaller ball, called the jack. The "woods" have a bias, are flattened so as to be slightly elliptical; considerable skill is required to allow for this bias.' (PP, p.295) 'Flat green bowls, though not a local pub game, is played in some of the parks, organised mostly by church groups . . .' (PP, p.297) 'Women also play bowls — but not on pub greens. This is important. The games described later . . . [in the chapter on "Sports, Games and Gambling"] — cards, dominoes, darts — are

vault and taproom games [i.e. played in "men only" bars], and so only played by men — exceptions being landlady and barmaid, to whom vault and taproom are not tabu.' (PP, p. 298 — and see notes to the 'Drinking' section below) 'They knew I was there, of course, because I had to go on the green. I would have spent a great deal of time, talking, joking with them — one of them probably said, "We'll chuck one of the bowls at you", and so on.' (HS)

66. From notes in Tom Harrisson's handwriting: 'Bolton Wanderers. 20/3. Fair crowd. 2/- seats: 22 bowlers, 32 trilbies (1 in plus-fours — doesn't watch game), 19 caps, 6 bare head, 5 lads, 1 woman (Eton crop, age 30). 1/- seats: 14 bowlers, 10 trilbies, c110 caps, 20 bare (most young), 3 women. A constable in bowler. Nag's Head barmen in bowler (1) & trilby (1). Moneylender in trilby, glass, stick (only one seen) stands by policemen. A Bowler is Hilden's[?] Garage Attendant. Remarks: First part — "Hit 'im", "No use at all", "Nicely", "Nicely", "Nicely", "Come on, Andy", "Start again" — foul at start. Shouts. A little man rushes up from bar, not having seen, & yells "Nasty. Nasty." "What a bloody shot." "Look at 'im — he's bow-legged — he's like a bludy black Minorca — a cross with a Leghorn. If I had a young one by him, I'd 'a drowned it." "They're not alive to the movements, that's the trouble. They stand there waiting."' (M-O)

71. With this photograph, there has been a slight double exposure, caused by a partial failure in the camera's film carriage mechanism.

Parks

74. Taken from the roof of what was then the museum in Merehall Park. Davenport Street is in among the mills in the middle distance.

75. This and the remaining photographs in this section were all taken in Queen's Park. No children's slide in a public park would be as high now.

Drinking

'I drink beer to keep me fit it do's the stummick good, and there is only one good reason I Drink Beer it is because I cannot eat it.' (Letter to local paper, quoted in PP, p.26) 'In Worktown more people spend more time in public houses than they do in any other buildings except private houses and work-places.' 'Sixteen per cent of all pub-goers are women.' (PP, pp.17 & 106) In 1936, there were 304 pubs in Bolton, with an average of 62 drinkers per pub (PP, pp.67 & 110). '3,000,000 gallons a year shared out amongst 20,000 Worktown pub-goers works out at a consumption of over 3 pints per head per day.' 'If we take a very low estimate of 150,000 pub visits per week in Worktown — nearly eight million a year — we find that the probability of the ordinary drinker getting "had up" after an evening in the

pub is one in 60,000. If he goes to the pub five nights a week it might, at that rate, take him two centuries before he was had up for being drunk.' (PP, pp.111 & 222/3)

80. 'There was one customer in the pub at this time (out of hours). Being a carter he recalled the good old times when carters were allowed a pint free or half price at all pubs round Worktown, to encourage stabling. And he told of how he himself had often gone out in his working clothes when hard up, and going into a pub would order a pint, and keep rushing to the door and shouting: "Whoa lad," and "Steady lass," etc., though his horse had been at home in the stables for an hour or two, thus letting an imaginary pal get him free drinks. He also told of a boss who when engaging him told him that he had been very pleased with a carter who had just left, because he was a teetotaller. However, when he took this carter's ex-horse out, it "pulled-in" of its own accord at six different pubs on the way to the next town.' (PP, p.210)

81. 'Despite the increasing popularity of darts, dominoes are still the most popular pub game.' (PP, p.301) And see the notes to p.64 above.

82. Taken in the Joiner's Hotel (now demolished to make way for shops) in the town centre. '. . . the woman's place in the pub is that part of it which is a home from home, a better home from ordinary worker's home, where — the only time in worker life in Worktown — you don't have to do any more than order someone else to serve your physiological need or wish. And, as usual, the woman's part is the one of cleanness, ashtrays, no random saliva, few or no spittoons. The vault [bar] is the place where men are men. In the lounge [bar] they are women's men, with collar studs. For that, as usual, they must pay another penny.' (PP, pp.106/7) Story about a local policeman, nicknamed 'Thirsty': He goes in the taproom, and sends his wife in the parlour, paying the waiter-on for her drinks. (This, the general custom, sometimes results in the husband finding that he has to pay for a big round for his wife's friends, which causes trouble.) Thirsty, although far better off than most of the pub-goers, only pays for mild for his wife, and the cheapest mild at that. She, however, has an arrangement with the waiter-on, so that when her husband orders and pays for her gill [half-pint], she has a Guinness fetched for her and pays the extra from her housekeeping money. This habit is widespread.' (PP, p.146)

83. Another town centre pub. '90 per cent of pub regulars don't walk more than 300 yards to get to their usual pubs.' (PP, p.33)

84. 'It's a vault — what some people called "the sawdust". It's not a room where women go. You see that fellow with his hand up, he's putting his hand up because he doesn't want to be identified. He'd be possibly unemployed, but looking at him, and gathering his age, he'd be possibly get-

ting money off Assistance Board. Now if the Assistance Board at that time found out that he were frittering money away on a vessel — they were only 2½d a gill then [1p a half-pint] — they'd stop his money. They were so keen at that time, very keen about that.' (HG) 'You can do almost anything you bloody well like in the vault, short of shitting on the place.' (Quoted in PP, p.105) In the Mass-Observation Archive, there is the following report, written by Humphrey Spender at the time, of an encounter in another pub. (As he says on p.16, '. . . when something difficult or embarrassing occurred, one tended to revert to stereotype . . . My rather pompous response to the publican must have been pretty insufferable; and it's painful to read now. However much I tried, I could not hide characteristics of myself that I would have preferred to keep hidden.') 'I was standing at a counter which gave a view on to a long row of drinkers standing at an opposite counter. The pub was very crowded and those serving drinks were sufficiently busy to keep them from paying much attention to what their customers were doing. My viewfinder was suddenly blocked by a large blue waistcoat and an aggressive voice said "What do you think you're doing? My customers don't want any photographs taken in here, nor do I. It's usual to ask the manager's permission." "I'm very sorry, may I have your permission?" "No, certainly not," and he was interrupted by having to serve some more drinks. Shortly afterwards he came back and I said "Now that I know you are the manager, can I have your permission to take a picture of the barman there, waiting with the tray — I shan't include any of your customers." "I've said before I won't have any photographs taken in here; my customers don't want it. What's more, before you leave you're going to destroy the films you've already taken." I put a protective hand over my camera and said "It's a pity I'll have to go without buying another drink." "I wouldn't serve you. Come on, destroy those films or I'll fetch a policeman." "Oh is there any law in England which prevents me from taking photographs in public houses?" "You needn't talk to me in that semi-educated way. You won't go until I've fetched a policeman", and he walked with me to the door, which he blocked, saying, "Destroy those films." "Well, let's fetch the policeman and see what the English law has to say about it." "Anyway," said Frank, "If you go on blocking that exit we can summon you for assault." The manager then went out and started beckoning for a policeman, who arrived in about 3 minutes. A sympathetic long-faced man who was completely dazed by the complaint and obviously didn't know the answer to my question — does the English law forbid me to take photographs inside a public house? The manager blustered and talked about forcing me to destroy the films, called me again semi-educated, to which I said my education on English law seemed sounder

than his. Included in a mass of personal insults I remember saying I certainly hadn't wanted a photograph of him and he said he wouldn't allow me in the place again. The manager kept on emphasising the point that his customers didn't want it known that they were in there. So I asked him if the place was so shady that they should be so nervous about exposing their presence. The policeman asked me why I was photographing, implying that the manager had a right to forbid publication. I said I had no intention of publishing anything and anyhow probably only had a picture of the manager's stomach which I didn't very much care about; that I was photographing entirely for my own pleasure, life in an industrial town. The manager then realised he was losing valuable time and went back to scenes of righteous indignation inside the pub. The policeman laughed and jerked his thumb into the pub, saying the manager was a queer customer.'

85. See note to p.45. 'If you come out of a pub at half past ten and stand on the flags outside a policeman'll move you on.' (Quoted in PP, p.327) 'This were a pub that during the war you could get anything. If you were stuck for razor blades, go in the Flag, and somebody would sell them you. Anything that were short.' (HG)

86. Town centre tea-room.

87. 'The secretary [of the local Temperance Union] holds meetings on the Town Hall steps. An observer's report says: Three men come together on the steps of the Town Hall. Speaker is a man of 55–60. They gather a group of 8 men, 1 woman. Speaker says, 'You hear of men who say they can drink 14 pints. Is there anyone who can say he is capable of knowing what he is doing at all by that stage . . . Can you deny that it is a waste of money when you have ceased to have any knowledge of the supposed enjoyment? . . .'' etc. (PP, p.318 — observer's dots) 'The origins of the national Temperance Movement were in this area.' (PP, p.315)

Elections

88. Farnworth 'abuts on and is in many senses part of Worktown'. (BR, p.89) The by-election was held in January 1938. The Labour candidate, George Tomlinson, defeated the National Government (Conservative) candidate, Herbert Ryan, by 24,298 votes to 16,835. Bolton itself had two MPs, both Conservative.

89 a–c. The Labour meeting was held at the Empire Cinema, Farnworth. In (a) and (b), the speaker is George Tomlinson; in (c), the Labour leader, Clement Attlee. 'When George Tomlinson stood for election there, his job actually was selling home-brewed beer. He used to go round Farnworth with a cart and everybody loved him. He wasn't a very well-educated fellow but, by crikey, when he spoke he were the best speaker I heard of all the lot.' (HG)

He became Minister of Education after the war. 'I didn't think a lot about Atlee. His voice was peculiar. He had a tendency sometimes to hurry his subject up. I don't know why he were like that. I think he had a voice that grated on your ears. It was like a piercing voice, I thought afterwards. I didn't go a bundle for him . . . We did have one Labour speaker come up at that time, and I'm not kidding, he were drunk as a monkey. I said, "This fellow's drunk" — I didn't say that, I said "He's pissed!" And he were. And you don't like that, do you? You see, I thought that these fellows who were speaking on behalf of the working class had great haloes round their heads. I very soon came undone about that.' (HG)

89d. This meeting is probably one held in the Co-op Hall, and not the one advertised in the upper photograph on p.88. 'I never went to any of them. I didn't waste my time, to be quite honest with you.' (HG)

92. Meeting outside the ILP (Independent Labour Party) headquarters. 'At that precise time, they had a very strong ILP faction in Farnworth — a lot stronger than what the Labour Party were. But there were no quibbling about which side they were on when the crunch came and there were a possibility of an MP they fancied and liked. They voted Labour.' (HG)

93. Labour canvasser on a council estate in Farnworth.

94. 'This is the way women dressed when I were a kid. This is the way my mother used to take us out. She'd be going a long distance or the weather'd be inclement. That's why she'd have a full shawl on. But generally they'd just wear a small shawl which covered the shoulders.' (HG) See also pp.36 & 98. 'Some sorts of clothes have almost disappeared. For older women, the black shawl worn over the head was standard in the thirties . . . In 1960 only one was seen. . . A stay-a-bed outsider of the thirties might be woken anywhere in Worktown by the sound of metal-shod wooden clogs upon the cobbled streets, going to the mills before daylight. Tonight the cobbles, millions of them, are the same as ever; but clogs are becoming a rarity.' (BR, p.32)

99. The children wore hats coloured according to the party they were supporting. Allen and (Mrs) Wright were elected for Labour in Bolton West; but the overall result in the Bolton municipal election for 1937 was announced by the Bolton Evening News as 'An Overwhelming Win for the Tories'. Including aldermen, the Conservatives had 56 seats, Labour 16, Liberals 16, and Independents 4.

Blackpool

Blackpool is 37 miles from Bolton. During the thirties, the Corporation claimed that there were up to eight million visitors in one year (BR, p.143). These came from all over the United Kingdom, but mainly from the industrial cities of Northern England and the Midlands. 'See, it were cheap. And it were always a lovely beach, and the sea were lovely, everything like that. You never had any scruffy water, always nice and clean. I used to come back with a suntan, anyway, from Blackpool. I used to go with my wife — she went on the train with my daughter, and I used to go on a push-bike after signing on at dole. And I used to come home on a Wednesday to sign on at dole; and I used to come home on Friday to sign on at dole and get my pay, and go back up Friday night — cycle back again. We just had lodgings, no board, the cheapest we could find. We brought our own stuff. In them days, people like my wife would go in the kitchen and cook it. Or if the landlady were a nice woman, she'd cook the breakfast and bring it in, and no charge for you. But you bought everything for yourself — your own tea, your own sugar; the only thing you didn't take were water. You were quite close to front, by the way. All those house have gone now, on Blackpool front where we used to go and stay. But wherever you stayed in Blackpool, these cheap lodging houses where we used to go to, they were quite close to front. So wherever you went, and we went quite a few years with my daughter, you wouldn't be above fifty yards from the front — possibly have a row of houses in front of where you lived and the sea.' (HG) 'I'm not savin' oop twelve bloody months for t' sake a gooing away fer a week. Wife's always asking what I do wi' me overtime, and I towd 'er — why, I bloody well spend it, what dost think — and she says — Tha owt t' 'ave more bloody sense.' (Quoted in PP, p.24)

105. In the distance is Blackpool Tower, built in the late nineteenth century. 'It was the time when architects were throwing up the Crystal Palace, the Forth Bridge and the Eiffel Tower, steel-girder skeletons, air and glitter between; symbols of the last iron age ... The height of the Tower to the top of the flagstaff was fixed at 518 feet 9 inches (above sea-level).' (BR, p.144)

109. 'There were three or four men around the machine playing on three of the arms. Observer went and joined in on the other arm. There is a revolving plate on which articles are placed, and by inserting a penny, the player can swing out an arm from the centre of the plate, and attempt to knock the articles down the chute. Normally this is a fairly difficult operation, but if two play together, and by careful timing a jam can be produced, forcing several articles down the delivery chute. When Observer started playing one of the men warned him not to take his arm out too far. In the next quarter of an hour the Observer, for the expenditure of 3d, had won 2 sixpenny packets of cigarettes, one fourpenny packet of weights [Player's Weights?], two egg-cups, three "Smallest Receiving Sets in the World", a 2d bar of Nestlés chocolate and a pocket mirror. The other men playing had similar wins... [Next morning] Observer

was at the same place and saw two of the same men at work on the machine... One man said that he and two pals had cleared the board of cigarettes in half an hour, for the cost of about sixpence... While Observer was there in the morning the refill man came round to replenish the supply. Asked him why he didn't put any more 1/– packets out. "Not while you boys are about."...' (M-O)

111. HS: 'What Tom was fascinated with there, was all the girls dancing together.' HG: 'Oh yes, this were quite a regular thing.'

115. There are records in the Archive showing how little people bathed. For example, at eleven o'clock one 'bright and warm' August morning, on a quarter-mile stretch of beach, there were 63 people in the water and 8,000 on the beach; and one 'sunny, windy' afternoon at the beginning of September, on a half-mile stretch, there were two in the water and 6,200 on the beach.

116. 'Colonel Barker, the army officer who was discovered to be a woman, was displayed in a pit; round the top people moved in an endless stream throughout the day. Down there, two single beds were separated by a pedestrian crossing, dotted lines between that then novel subject of bawdy jokes, orange Belisha Beacons. In one bed lay the portly frame of the Colonel in a sort of nightshirt; in the other a young girl in a flimsy. Beside the young girl generally lay a huge spotted Dalmatian dog. Under the Colonel's bed there usually lay a bottle of whisky. As the 1937 season proceeded, twelve hours a day in bed being abused and spat at from above, put over 20 lb. on the Colonel's weight.' (BR, p.149) The impresario responsible for this exhibition was one of Blackpool's most famous showmen, Luke Gannon, who is quoted as saying: 'I always say that you can divide the public like this — 50% certifiable, 30% on the brink, and the other 20% living on the others.' (M-O) In defence of the words on his sign, 'I am taking this step for the woman I love', he said: 'I suppose you think I took them from King Edward. The police thought that too, and at Whit many people were saying that I was commercialising the pathetic words of his late majesty. But what would you say if I told you that I wrote those words three years ago? I was able to show the police a receipt for my order for those words to be printed by the Gazette office. They were staggered when I said to them, now don't you think it is the King who should be apologising to me for using the words?' (M-O) He also commented: 'The Belisha beacons are a sign of futuristic love. People go so fast now in their courting and the beacon is a sign for them to pull up and go a bit slower.' (M-O)

117. 'In the end of September the holiday rush slows. Then the year is marvellously extended by the light in autumn of "Illuminations", switched on by royalty, featuring mainly fairy-tale mythology scenes, jugglers and tumblers

also and the Blackpool Rejuvenator Machine which takes in illuminated old people and turns them out the other end as illuminated young people. Brilliant tableaux wall off the dark sea behind; the piers are ill-lit, but have searchlights sweeping to land. Huge bluebirds flutter over the road, avenued with pillars like piled clown-caps...' (Geographical Magazine, April 1938, pp.403/4)

Funeral

All the photographs in this last section are of one funeral, that of John Shaw who lived in Davenport Street, and died on 17 September 1937. 'Observer was at the graveside at 2 p.m.... Two gravediggers dressed in floppy felt hats, brown overalls, and thick trousers, leggings and clogs of wood, the trousers and leggings being in addition protected with canvas cloth, stood near. A third workman in the same dress but without overalls stood at the bottom of the main path and supervised the carrying of the coffin to the grave... The mourners got out of the cars and formed a procession four abreast as they came up the hill. First came the gravedigger, then the coffin, borne by six men, then the mourners, 21 men and 8 women. All wore black or navy blue suits, black ties. The coffin was carried to the grave and lowered in. Each of the mourners was given a white chrysanthemum by one of the gravediggers. The ceremony consisted in an address read by a middle-aged man with black hair. Observer did not notice any earth was thrown on the coffin, and certainly no words were spoken by anyone apart from this address, which was original and moving, and well delivered by the speaker. Most of the men had tears in their eyes; one or two had obviously been weeping a great deal previous to the funeral. Observer could not get down all of the address, but the following fragments give an idea of its content [the dots are the observer's]. "Our friend has entered into the eternal rest... Death comes as a soothing anodyne... The penalty of life is death... The clouds over him will weep for us... the flowers will grow in the earth where he lies, and the earth will produce a harvest rich with fruits of the earth... This is the only immortality that we recognise — the immortality of the great ones of the world... May the flowers bloom over his head... Farewell, John James Shaw! A long farewell!" The mourners each gave a last look into the grave and then moved off. At least 10 people who were not mourners stood near the whole time, including two women who kept peeping between the gravestones.' (M-O)

120. 'Possibly these women have come out of the next street, which were Kent Street, which is a totally different street altogether. Kent Street were a poor area.' (HG)

123. On the stone at the head of John Shaw's grave, here, in Heaton Cemetary, the inscription reads: 'ONE OF THE BEST'.